easy vegan

easy vegan

simple recipes for healthy eating

RYLAND
PETERS
& SMALL

LONDON NEW YORK

Designers Iona Hoyle and
Sonya Nathoo
Commissioning Editor Julia Charles
Picture Research Emily Westlake
Production Toby Marshall
Art Director Leslie Harrington
Publishing Director Alison Starling

Indexer Hilary Bird

First published in 2010
by Ryland Peters & Small
20–21 Jockey's Fields
London WC1R 4BW
and
Ryland Peters & Small, Inc.
519 Broadway, 5th Floor
New York, NY10012

www.rylandpeters.com

10 9 8 7 6 5 4 3 2

UK ISBN 978 1 84597 958 4
US ISBN 978 1 84597 959 1

A CIP record for this book is available
from the British Library.

Library of Congress Cataloging-in-
Publication Data
Easy vegan : simple recipes for healthy
eating.
   p. cm.
 Includes index.
 ISBN 978-1-84597-959-1
 1. Vegan cookery. I. Ryland Peters &
Small.
 TX837.E27 2010
 641.5'636--dc22

2009049514

Printed in China

Notes

• All spoon measurements are level,
unless otherwise specified.

• Ovens should be preheated to the
specified temperature. Recipes in this
book were tested using a regular oven.
If using a fan-assisted oven, follow
the manufacturer's instructions for
adjusting temperatures.

• When a recipe calls for the grated
peel/zest of citrus fruit, buy unwaxed
fruit and wash well before using. If
you can only find treated fruit, scrub
well in warm soapy water and rinse
before using.

contents

simply good food

This is the perfect book for anyone who is following a vegan diet or preparing meals for vegan family and friends. Whether it's to boost and maintain health with a pure diet, or for reasons of conscience and personal choice, vegan food is ever popular. *Easy Vegan* is full of exciting recipes, inspired by many different styles of cooking from around the world, all of which cut out animal products. They are quick and easy to prepare and rely on real food and ingredients, rather than specialist, often difficult-to-source vegan substitutes.

Included are fresh ideas for soups, snacks and light meals, salads, hot dishes, sweet things, and drinks. The recipes show just how easy it is to use fresh herbs, spices, seasonings, and condiments sourced from all over the globe to pack plenty of flavor and vitality into your vegan cooking. Try an exotic tagine from North Africa that uses fiery harissa paste to add zing; a fresh, herbed salad packed full of nutritious grains from the Middle East; a tasty stir-fried noodle dish from China or Japan; a satisfyingly spicy curry from India; or a simple recipe from Spain, Italy, or France that showcases simple vegetables at their best to create a dish full of Mediterranean sunshine.

For more detailed information on maintaining good health whilst enjoying a vegan diet visit these specialist websites—www.americanvegan.org or www.vegansociety.com.

soups

garlic and chile rice soup with spring greens

1 tablespoon vegetable oil

2 teaspoons sesame oil

2 garlic cloves, chopped

4 scallions/spring onions, finely chopped

2 teaspoons finely grated fresh ginger

1 small red chile, seeded and thinly sliced

½ cup/100 g long-grain white rice

6 cups/1.5 litres vegetable stock

1 tablespoon soy sauce

1 bunch of spring greens, roughly shredded

1 small bunch of cilantro/ fresh coriander, chopped

ground white pepper, to taste

Serves 2

This is a substantial soup—really more of a light stew. Boiled rice soups are popular in many Asian countries, especially China where they are called congees. They are often eaten for breakfast, but are an acquired taste as the rice is boiled until it breaks down to form a rather viscous white "porridge." Spring greens can be the fresh, young outer leaves of brassicas such as cabbage. They work very nicely with the simple Asian seasonings used here.

Put the oils in a saucepan and set over high heat. Add the garlic and scallions/spring onions and cook until the garlic is turning golden and just starting to burn. Add the ginger, chile, and rice to the pan and stir-fry in the garlic-infused oil for 1 minute. Add the stock and soy sauce and bring to a boil.

Cover with a lid and cook over low heat for 30 minutes, until the rice is soft and the soup has thickened. Add the spring greens and cook for a further 5 minutes, until they turn emerald green and are tender. Ladle the soup into warmed serving bowls, sprinkle the cilantro/coriander over the top and season to taste with pepper.

miso with ramen noodles and stir-fried vegetables

3 tablespoons red miso paste

1 tablespoon light soy sauce

½ teaspoon white sugar

6 cups/1.5 litres vegetable stock

7 oz./200 g ramen or thin egg noodles

1 tablespoon light olive oil

2 teaspoons sesame oil

2 teaspoons finely sliced fresh ginger

2 shallots, thinly sliced

2 leeks, julienned

7 oz./200 g Savoy cabbage leaves, finely shredded

7 oz./200 g red cabbage, finely shredded

Serves 4

Hearty Japanese soups are often full of earthy cold-weather vegetables. The broths are made with a base of simple stock and miso. This prepared, soya bean paste is the most essential Japanese ingredient with a very strong "unami" (savory) flavor. Easily found in the Asian foods aisle at the supermarket, it will keep for ages in your refrigerator. The noodles, although common in Japan, are Chinese wheat-based noodles and, when bought dried, are a very handy pantry staple.

Combine the miso, soy sauce, sugar, and stock in a large saucepan set over medium heat and warm until the miso has completely dissolved. Keep warm over low heat. Cook the noodles according to the package instructions. Drain well and put into warmed serving bowls.

Put the oils in a wok or large skillet/frying pan set over high heat. Add the ginger and shallots and cook for just a few seconds to flavor the oil. Add the leeks and cabbage and stir-fry for 2 minutes, until the vegetables are crisp and glistening with oil.

Ladle the warm miso mixture over the noodles and top with the stir-fried vegetables. Serve immediately.

chickpea, cherry tomato, and green bean minestrone

2 tablespoons olive oil

1 onion, chopped

2 garlic cloves, chopped

14-oz./400-g can chickpeas, rinsed and drained

4 oz./115 g green beans, sliced on the angle

12 cherry tomatoes

a handful of fresh flat-leaf parsley, roughly chopped

6 cups/1.5 litres vegetable stock

3–4 oz./100 g whole-wheat spaghetti, broken into short lengths

2 large handfuls of arugula/rocket

½ cup/50 g vegan Parmesan substitute (such as Parma) or nutritional yeast (optional)

sea salt and freshly ground black pepper

crusty bread, to serve

Serves 4

Minestrone soup is often thought of as cold weather food but this version has summer written all over it and is packed with fresh cherry tomatoes and green beans as well as nutritious chickpeas. A few handfuls of arugula/rocket give a peppery bite and fresh taste that lightens the soup.

Put the oil in a large saucepan set over medium heat. Add the onion, partially cover with a lid, and cook for 4–5 minutes, stirring often, until softened. Add the garlic and cook for 1 minute. Add the chickpeas, green beans, tomatoes, parsley, stock, and spaghetti and bring to a boil.

Reduce the heat and let simmer for about 40 minutes, stirring often, until the pasta is cooked and the soup has thickened. Season to taste with salt and pepper.

Just before serving, add the arugula/rocket and gently stir until it wilts into the soup. Ladle into warmed serving bowls and sprinkle Parma over the top, if using. Serve immediately with crusty bread.

Variation:

Try making this delicious soup with different vegetables. Zucchini/courgettes and carrots are a nice addition but remember that both take a little longer to cook so dice them very finely before adding to the soup with the other vegetables. A pinch of smoky Spanish paprika (pimentón) will add a slightly different flavor.

sweet potato and coconut soup with Thai pesto

1 tablespoon light olive oil

1 lb./450 g sweet potato, peeled and chopped into chunks

1 red onion, chopped

1 tablespoon Thai red curry paste*

2 cups/500 ml vegetable stock

2 cups/500 ml coconut milk

For the Thai pesto:

⅔ cup/100 g unsalted peanuts, lightly toasted

2 garlic cloves, chopped

2 teaspoons finely grated fresh ginger

2 large green chiles, seeded and chopped

a small bunch of cilantro/ fresh coriander

a large handful of fresh mint leaves

a large handful of fresh basil leaves

2 tablespoons light soy sauce

2 tablespoons freshly squeezed lime juice

1 tablespoon soft light brown sugar

Serves 4

Sweet potatoes make an excellent ingredient for soups. When blended they take on a velvety, creamy texture. Here, their sweetness is cut through with a spicy Thai-style pesto, which really brings this soup to life.

Put the oil in a heavy-based saucepan and set over medium heat. Add the sweet potato and onion, partially cover with a lid, and cook for 15 minutes, stirring often, until they are soft and just starting to turn golden. Increase the heat to high, add the curry paste, and stir-fry with the sweet potato for 3–4 minutes so that the paste cooks and becomes fragrant. Add the stock and coconut milk and bring to a boil. Transfer the mixture to a food processor or blender and whizz until smooth. Return the blended soup to a clean saucepan.

To make the pesto, put all of the ingredients in a food processor or blender and whizz, occasionally scraping down the sides of the bowl, until you have a chunky green paste and the ingredients are all evenly chopped. Gently reheat the soup, then ladle into warmed serving bowls. Top with a generous spoonful of Thai pesto to serve.

*Note: Be aware that some brands of Thai red curry paste contain traces of seafood and are not suitable for a vegan diet. However, there are many vegan-friendly brands available so just be sure to read the ingredients carefully before you choose one.

Italian bean and vegetable soup

5 cups/1.2 litres vegetable stock

1 onion, chopped

2 garlic cloves, crushed

2 carrots, diced

2 cups/150 g chopped mushrooms

2 zucchini/courgettes, diced

3 cups/700 g passata (Italian sieved tomatoes)

14-oz./410-g can cannellini beans, drained and rinsed

1¼ cups/150 g shredded green cabbage

3 tablespoons chopped fresh basil

sea salt and freshly ground black pepper

whole-wheat bread, to serve

Serves 6

This simple yet hearty soup is delicious served with a large chunk of stoneground, whole-wheat bread.

Put about 4 tablespoons of the stock in a large flameproof casserole or saucepan and set over medium heat. Add the onion and garlic, replace the lid and cook for 5 minutes until soft. Add the carrots, mushrooms, and zucchini/courgettes and stir. Season and cook for 2 minutes. Stir in the passata, add the remaining stock, and bring to a simmer, then cover and cook for 10 minutes.

Add the beans and cabbage, re-cover the pan and simmer for a further 10 minutes. Stir in the basil and adjust the seasoning to taste. Ladle into warmed serving bowls and serve with whole-wheat bread.

Variation:

Instead of the cannellini beans, you can use the same amount of canned chickpeas in this recipe.

gazpacho

9 oz./250 g ripe, red tomatoes, blanched, skinned and finely diced

½ red or white onion, finely chopped

4 oz./100 g cucumber, peeled and finely diced

1 green bell pepper, halved, seeded, and diced (optional)

1 tablespoon tomato paste/purée

2 garlic cloves, chopped

1 cup/60 g cubed stale bread

3 tablespoons Pedro Ximenez vinegar, or sherry vinegar plus 1 tablespoon sweet sherry

1 tablespoon extra virgin olive oil

sea salt and freshly ground black pepper

For the olive ice cubes:

green olive ice cubes

12 green Spanish olives, stuffed with almonds if available

chilled sparkling water

an ice cube tray (optional)

Serves 4–6

Gazpacho is the famous iced tomato soup from Spain. It is even better made with sweetly mellow Pedro Ximenez vinegar, produced from one of Spain's most distinguished sweet wines. It is found in Hispanic grocers or good wine merchants. The flavor of the tomatoes is important so do use good-quality, vine-ripened varieties. The olive ice cubes are optional but look very attractive and are a nice touch when serving the soup at a dinner party. Plain ice cubes are fine if preferred.

To make the olive ice cubes, start the day before. Set 12 stuffed olives in an ice cube tray. Fill it with sparkling water and freeze. Store the ice cubes in the freezer until ready to serve.

Put the prepared tomatoes, onion, cucumber, bell pepper, and the tomato paste/purée in a food processor or blender. Add the garlic, bread cubes, half the vinegar, all the oil, and about 1¾ cups/400 ml water. Purée the soup continuously until it becomes a smooth, brick-red mixture. Add salt and pepper to taste, then add the remaining vinegar. Blend again.

Pour into 4–6 stemmed glasses, each with 2–3 olive ice cubes: the olives act as additional seasoning. Serve immediately.

zucchini and corn soup

3 tablespoons extra virgin olive oil

2 onions, sliced

3 zucchini/courgettes, quartered lengthwise, then sliced

10 oz./300 g potatoes, diced

4 garlic cloves, sliced

2 ears of corn, kernels scraped off with a knife

1 teaspoon ground cumin

1 red chile, seeded and sliced

4 cups/1 litre vegetable stock

a handful of chopped cilantro/fresh coriander, to garnish

Tabasco sauce, to taste

sea salt

Serves 4

This is inspired by the cuisine of America's South-west. The chilli content is rather conservative, but you can spice it up as much as you like. The suggested trimmings are optional but delicious. You can also purée the soup for a thicker, more chowder-like consistency if liked.

Heat the oil in a large saucepan. Add the onions, zucchini/courgettes, potatoes and some salt and cook over high heat until beginning to brown, about 5 minutes.

Add the garlic, corn, cumin, and chile and cook, stirring continuously, for 1 minute more. Add the stock and 1 cup/250 ml water, then add salt to taste. Bring to a boil, then lower the heat and simmer gently until the potatoes are tender, 15–20 minutes. Set aside for at least 30 minutes.

When ready to serve, reheat the soup. Ladle into warmed serving bowls and top each with a sprinkling of chopped cilantro/coriander and a dash of Tabasco. Serve immediately.

butternut squash soup
with allspice and pine nuts

1 medium butternut squash, halved lengthwise and seeded

2 tablespoons safflower/sunflower oil

1 large leek, trimmed and chopped

1 bay leaf

a few black peppercorns, crushed

4–5 allspice berries, crushed

2¾ cups/600 ml vegetable stock

¾ cup/60 g pine nuts, toasted in a dry skillet/frying pan

crusty bread, to serve

Serves 4

Squashes and allspice are native to the Americas and pine nuts have been gathered in the deserts of the south-west for at least a thousand years. This is a quintessentially American soup, popular in both north and south. What better comfort on a cold day? The key to this soup is the light spicing and the roasting of the butternut squash to bring out the best of its sweet flavor.

Preheat the oven to at 375ºF (190ºC) Gas 5.

Put the butternut squash halves flesh-side down on a non-stick baking sheet. Roast in the preheated oven for about 45 minutes, until tender. Remove from the oven and, using a spoon, scoop the flesh out of the skins into a bowl. Discard the skins.

Put the butter into a large saucepan and melt over low/medium heat. Add the leek, bay leaf, peppercorns, and allspice and fry gently until the leek begins to soften. Add the butternut squash, stock, and 4 cups/1 litre water. Bring to a boil, reduce the heat, and simmer for about 10 minutes, or until the leeks are very soft.

Remove the bay leaf and transfer the soup to a blender or food processor. Add the pine nuts and blend until smooth, working in batches if necessary. Return the soup to the saucepan and reheat. Serve hot with crusty bread.

summer vegetable and lemon broth

2 tablespoons olive oil

1 lemon

1 onion, chopped

3 tablespoons chopped fresh flat-leaf parsley, plus extra to serve

1 lb./450 g zucchini/courgettes, sliced

10 oz./300 g fava/broad beans (podded weight)

3¼ cups/800 ml vegetable stock

sea salt and freshly ground black pepper

For the lemon and thyme oil:

2 lemons

2 fresh thyme or lemon thyme sprigs

1 cup/250 ml extra virgin olive oil

Serves 4

This soup is very useful if you have a vegetable garden, as both zucchini/courgettes and fava/broad beans are easy to grow. It's also often the case that you end up with a real glut of them. To make the broth more substantial you can add a scoop of risotto rice at the same time as the beans and a little more stock to compensate. If you are using large beans you might want to slip them out of their pale green jackets. The lemony oil adds an acidic bite to the soup but is optional.

To make the lemon and thyme oil, remove the lemon peel using a potato peeler, making sure you leave behind the bitter white pith. Put the peel, thyme, and olive oil in a small saucepan and heat gently for 10 minutes. Remove from the heat and let cool. Season to taste. Transfer to a clean, lidded jar, seal, and store in the refrigerator for up to 2–3 days.

To make the soup, heat the olive oil in a large saucepan. Remove the peel from the lemon in one large piece so it's easy to find later and add it to the pan. Add the onion, parsley, and zucchini/courgettes, cover with a lid, and cook over low heat for about 8 minutes, stirring occasionally, until it begins to soften.

Remove the lemon peel. Add the fava/broad beans and stock, season well with salt and pepper, and return to the heat for a further 20 minutes.

Transfer a quarter of the soup to a blender, liquidize until smooth, then stir back into the soup. Check the seasoning and add lemon juice to taste.

Divide the soup between serving bowls, drizzle with lemon and thyme oil, and serve with extra parsley and a fresh grinding of black pepper.

roast eggplant and red bell pepper soup with basil oil

1 large eggplant/aubergine

4 red bell peppers

2 fresh thyme sprigs

1 garlic bulb, halved horizontally

2 tablespoons extra virgin olive oil

1 red onion, cut into wedges

2 cups/500 ml vegetable stock

1¼ cups/300 g passata (Italian sieved tomatoes)

a handful of fresh oregano leaves

sea salt and freshly ground black pepper

fresh basil leaves, to garnish

For the basil oil:

2 large handfuls fresh basil leaves

1 small garlic clove, chopped

¾ cup/195 ml extra virgin olive oil

sea salt and freshly ground black pepper

Serves 4–6

The smoky flavors of the roast eggplant/aubergine, bell peppers, and garlic make this soup really enticing. The basil oil makes a great addition to any tomato-based soup.

To make the basil oil, put the basil, garlic, a large pinch of salt, and some pepper in a food processor. Blend until roughly chopped. With the motor running, gradually trickle in the olive oil unti it is blended. Transfer to a clean, lidded jar, seal, and store in the refrigerator up to 1 week.

To make the soup, preheat the oven to 375ºF (190ºC) Gas 5. Put the whole eggplant/aubergine and bell peppers in a large roasting pan. Sandwich the thyme between the garlic halves, drizzle with the olive oil, then wrap in foil and add to the pan. Roast in the preheated oven for 35 minutes.

Remove the garlic from the oven, checking it is tender first, and set aside to cool. Remove the bell peppers, transfer to a plastic bag, seal, and let cool. Add the onion to the roasting pan (still containing the eggplant/aubergine) and roast for about 20 minutes, or until the eggplant/aubergine feels tender when pierced with a knife.

Meanwhile, peel the skins off the cooled bell peppers and discard. Transfer the flesh to a blender and liquidize with a third of the stock until smooth. Transfer to a saucepan. Squeeze out the soft flesh from inside the garlic cloves and add to the blender. Spoon the flesh of the eggplant/aubergine into the blender with the onion and another third of the stock. Blend until smooth, then add to the puréed peppers in the saucepan. Add the passata, oregano, and remaining stock and bring to a boil. Season to taste.

Ladle the soup into serving bowls, drizzle with basil oil and scatter with basil leaves.

snacks and light meals

spicy Cajun mixed nuts

5 oz./140 g unsalted cashews

5 oz./140 g shelled pecans

5 oz./140 g shelled pistachios

1 teaspoon cayenne pepper

1 teaspoon pimentón (Spanish smoked paprika)

½ teaspoon dried thyme

1 teaspoon fine sea salt

1 tablespoon soft brown sugar

1 tablespoon olive oil

a baking sheet lined with baking parchment

Serves 10–12

Cashews, pecans, and pistachios are listed in the ingredients here, but feel free to choose any nuts you like. Buy them in bulk and you will save money—they won't go to waste as this is a recipe you'll definitely want to make more than once!

Preheat the oven to 350°F (180°C) Gas 4.

Put all of the nuts in a large bowl. Add the cayenne pepper, paprika, thyme, salt, and sugar and mix to combine. Stir in the olive oil. Tip the nuts out onto the lined baking sheet, spreading them out into a single layer.

Bake in the preheated oven for 10 minutes, stirring about halfway through the cooking time. Let cool completely before spooning into serving bowls. The nuts are great served with drinks or as a snack. They will keep well for 7–10 days if stored in an airtight container.

Lebanese hot red pepper and walnut dip (muhammara)

1 cup/150 g shelled walnuts

6 tablespoons fresh white or brown bread crumbs

7 oz./200 g piquillo roasted red bell peppers

1 garlic clove, crushed

1 teaspoon *pimentón picante* (Spanish smoked hot paprika)

1 teaspoon ground cumin

1 tablespoon tomato paste/purée

1 tablespoon red wine vinegar

2 tablespoons pomegranate molasses*

6 tablespoons extra-virgin olive oil

fresh pomegranate seeds, to serve (optional)

sea salt and freshly ground black pepper

toasted pitta bread, or vegetable crudités, to serve

Serves 4–6

This deliciously exotic and spicy dip is easy to make and can be served warm or cold. Serve it with toasted pitta bread or fresh vegetable sticks for dipping.

Toast the walnuts in a dry skillet/frying pan for about 2 minutes, until fragrant. Set aside to cool.

Put the toasted walnuts and bread crumbs in a food processor and whizz until finely ground. Add the peppers and garlic and process until smooth and then add the pimentón, cumin, tomato paste/purée, vinegar, and pomegranate molasses. Season well with salt and pepper and blend again until the dip is smooth and creamy.

With the motor running, slowly pour in the olive oil until it is incorporated. If the mixture is too thick, add a few tablespoons of water or lemon juice. Serve sprinkled with fresh pomegranate seeds, if using. Cover and refrigerate until ready to serve.

*Note: This thick, fragrant, and tangy reduction of pomegranate juice is made by boiling the liquid until it becomes stick and syrupy. It's a key ingredient in traditional Middle Eastern cooking and has become an increasingly popular gourmet ingredient over the last few years. It is available from larger supermarkets and online retailers. If you can't find it, put ¾ cup/195 ml pomegranate juice in a small saucepan and bring to a boil. Reduce the heat to medium and simmer, uncovered, for about 6 minutes, until the juice is reduced to about 2 tablespoons. Set aside to cool and thicken before using.

smoked eggplant dip
(baba ghanoush)

2 lbs./1 kg eggplants/aubergines

about ⅔ cup/150 ml olive oil

2 garlic cloves, crushed

4 tablespoons tahini

freshly squeezed juice of 1–2 lemons,
or to taste

sea salt and freshly ground
black pepper

To serve:

1 tablespoon sweet paprika

3 tablespoons olive oil

2 tablespoon chopped fresh
flat-leaf parsley

toasted pitta bread or other flatbread,
to serve

Serves 4–6

This creamy dip can be served as part of a selection of little dishes or a simple appetizer/starter. Normally the dish is made from vegetables that have been roasted whole and the flesh scooped out. In this version, they are peeled, then sliced and roasted, so the result is much more mellow.

Preheat the oven to 400°F (200°C) Gas 6.

Trim the eggplants/aubergines, peel, then slice thickly. Arrange the slices on a baking sheet and brush both sides with olive oil. Roast in the preheated oven for about 20 minutes, until browning and soft, turning them once.

Remove from the oven and let cool for 5 minutes. Transfer to a food processor and add the garlic, tahini, and the juice of 1 lemon. Process until creamy, then taste and adjust the seasoning with salt, pepper, and more lemon juice.

Pour or spoon into a shallow dish. Mix the paprika with the 3 tablespoons olive oil and trickle it over the top of the baba ghanoush. Sprinkle with parsley and serve with strips of toasted pitta bread for dipping.

Note: For a softer garlic flavor, roast the garlic cloves whole and unpeeled with the eggplants/aubergines, then squeeze the soft flesh out of the skins and blend with the eggplants/aubergines.

Italian bean dip

2 cups/400 g dried fava/broad beans

1 freshly made bouquet garni of parsley, bay leaf, celery rib/stalk, and thyme

1 large onion, coarsely chopped

1 potato, unpeeled

4 garlic cloves, chopped

¼ cup/60 ml extra virgin olive oil, plus extra to drizzle

freshly squeezed juice of 1 lemon (4–5 tablespoons)

6 sprigs of fresh oregano, chopped

sea salt and freshly ground black pepper

toasted ciabatta or sourdough bread, to serve

Serves 4

All round the Mediterranean, fresh and dried peas, beans, and lentils are used in dips and spreads. Depending on the region and local ingredients, different herbs are used. The best fava/broad beans to use are the skinless type: they cook quickly, taste better and have a more delicate texture.

Soak the fava/broad beans for 4 hours or overnight in cold water. Drain, cover with cold water, bring to a boil, and simmer until tender. Drain again.

Put the beans in a large saucepan with the bouquet garni, onion, and potato and add 2 quarts/2 litres boiling water. Bring to a boil, boil hard for 10 minutes, reduce the heat and cook, part-covered for 1½–2 hours or until you can crush the beans easily with your thumbnail.

Drain the vegetables, reserving 2–3 tablespoons of liquid. Discard the bouquet garni. Working in batches if necessary, put the beans, potato, onion, and garlic in a food processor, with the olive oil, lemon juice, oregano, salt, and pepper. Blend in short bursts until you have a grainy but creamy purée.

Serve hot, warm, or cold as preferred, drizzled with olive oil and with toasted ciabatta on the side.

Greek yellow split pea purée

1½ cups/300 g yellow split peas
or Greek fava if available

2 onions, finely chopped

2 tablespoons capers, rinsed

5–6 tablespoons extra-virgin olive oil

freshly squeezed juice of 1 lemon

4–6 black olives

sea salt and freshly ground
black pepper

toasted pitta bread, to serve

Serves 6

This dip is always part of ameze in Greece. Authentic Greek "fava" (not to be confused with fava/broad beans) may look similar to yellow split peas, but they have a much sweeter taste—the best come from the Greek island of Santorini.

Soak the split peas in cold water for 1–2 hours. Drain, rinse, put in a saucepan and cover with 2 quarts/2 litres water. Bring to a boil and skim the surface until the cooking water is clear.

Add just over half the chopped onion and simmer, uncovered, for at least 1 hour, or until perfectly soft. Stir occasionally and add some hot water if needed. At the end of cooking, when the dish has the consistency of thick soup, add salt.

Transfer to a food processor or blender while it is still hot, process until smooth, then pour into a serving bowl immediately as it solidifies when cold.

Sprinkle the capers, black pepper, and the remaining onion over the top, drizzle with the olive oil and lemon juice, and pile the olives in the middle. Serve warm or at room temperature with strips of toasted pitta bread on the side for dipping.

hummus

¾ cup/150 g dried chickpeas or
1½ x 14-oz./410-g cans chickpeas,
drained and rinsed

¼ cup/60 ml freshly squeezed
lemon juice

1–2 garlic cloves

5 tablespoons tahini

½ teaspoon sea salt

extra virgin olive oil, for drizzling
(optional)

vegetable crudités and flatbreads,
to serve

Makes about 2⅓ cups/600 ml

Hummus is simple and fun to make at home. It's also versatile, as you can flavor it to suit your own taste. For an extra-special, creamy hummus, peel the skin from the cooked chickpeas, an arduous task, but you'll be amazed at the results.

If using dried chickpeas, soak them overnight or for at least 12 hours. Drain and put in a large saucepan. Cover with about 3 times the volume of water. Bring to a boil, reduce to a simmer, and cook for 1½ hours or until tender, topping up the water if necessary. Drain the chickpeas and reserve about 3 tablespoons of the cooking liquid. Let cool. (At this point you can rub the chickpeas to loosen the skins and discard.)

Put the cooked chickpeas in a food processor or blender with the lemon juice, garlic, tahini, and salt. Process to a smooth purée, adding some of the cooking liquid (or a little water if you are using canned chickpeas) to achieve the desired consistency. Serve drizzled with olive oil, if liked. The hummus will keep in the refrigerator for 5 days.

Variations:

Roast garlic hummus Preheat the oven to 350°F (180°C) Gas 4. Cut about ½ inch/1 cm off the top of a whole bulb of garlic and discard. Loosely wrap the garlic in foil and roast in the preheated oven for about 45 minutes until very soft. Let cool. Squeeze the soft garlic cloves out of their skins and add to the chickpeas when you purée them.

Grilled vegetable hummus On a charcoal grill or in a ridged stovetop grill pan, cook slices of red bell pepper, eggplant/aubergine, pumpkin, or zucchini/courgette that have been tossed with a little olive oil. Add to the chickpeas when you purée them.

Minted pea hummus Add ¾ cup/130 g cooked peas and 2 tablespoons chopped fresh mint to the chickpeas when you purée them.

guacamole

3 medium, ripe avocados,
halved, pitted, and peeled

2 tablespoons freshly squeezed
lime juice

1 small red onion, very finely chopped

1–2 green chiles, seeded and very
finely chopped

1 tomato, seeded and finely chopped

sea salt

bread sticks or plain tortilla chips,
to serve

Makes 2 cups/500 ml

This popular Mexican dip can be made in many ways. Here the recipe contains all the popular ingredients, but feel free to leave out any you don't like. You can adjust the quantity of chiles that you use according to your personal taste.

Put the avocado flesh in a bowl with the lime juice and crush to a rough purée with a fork (if you like a smooth purée, you can blend the avocado and lime juice together in a food processor or blender, then transfer to a bowl.)

Add the onion, chiles, and tomato and mix until combined. Season to taste with salt. Serve with bread sticks or tortilla chips on the side for dipping.

The guacamole will discolor quickly, so is best eaten on the day of making.

Variation:

Herbed guacamole Stir in 2 teaspoons each of finely fresh chopped cilantro/fresh coriander, mint, and parsley to the guacamole for a more pungent, refreshing dip.

artichoke tarator

2 slices of day-old bread,
crusts removed

6 canned artichoke hearts, drained

freshly squeezed juice of 1 lemon

3–4 garlic cloves, crushed

½ teaspoon sea salt

½ cup/70 g blanched almonds,
finely chopped

4 tablespoons extra virgin olive oil,
plus extra for drizzling

toasted slivered/flaked almonds,
to garnish (optional)

vegetable crudités, to serve

Makes about 2 cups/500 ml

Tarator is a fabulous garlic and nut dip, and this version has artichokes to make it extra special. Perfect as a dip with vegetable crudités—it goes especially well with endive. In Turkey it is served as a spooning sauce so do try it with grilled vegetables too.

Put the bread in a strainer/sieve and pour over boiling water. When cool enough to handle, squeeze out any excess water.

Chop the artichoke hearts and put them in a food processor or large pestle and mortar with the bread, lemon juice, garlic, salt, and almonds. Blend together, adding the oil slowly to combine.

To serve, drizzle with olive oil and scatter with the almonds, if using. Serve with a selection of vegetable crudités for dipping. The tarator will keep, covered, in the refrigerator for up to 3 days.

puy lentil and carrot pâté

½ cup/125 g Puy lentils

4 tablespoons olive oil

3 garlic cloves, finely chopped

1 onion, chopped

1 teaspoon coriander seeds, crushed

1 teaspoon cumin seeds, crushed

1 teaspoon fresh minced chile

2 large carrots, thickly sliced

¼ cup/60 ml vegetable stock

1 tablespoon tomato paste/purée

4 tablespoons chopped cilantro/
fresh coriander, plus extra leaves
to garnish

extra virgin olive oil, to drizzle

sea salt and freshly ground
black pepper

warmed flatbreads, to serve

Makes about 2½ cups/625 ml

The combination of lentil, carrot, and cilantro/fresh coriander gives a warming Turkish feel to this spread-like pâté. It is best served with toasted Middle-Eastern bread or Turkish pide.

Rinse the lentils with water then put them in a saucepan and cover with plenty of water. Bring to a boil, then reduce to a simmer and cook for 15 minutes. Drain and set aside.

Heat the olive oil in a heavy-based saucepan over medium heat. Add the garlic, onion, coriander and cumin seeds, chile, and carrots and cook, stirring continuously, for 5 minutes. Add the cooked lentils, stock, and tomato paste/purée. Reduce to a low simmer, cover and cook for about 15 minutes, stirring occasionally. Leave in the pan, covered, to cool.

Transfer the mixture to a food processor or blender and process to a thick purée. Season to taste with salt and pepper and stir in the cilantro/fresh coriander. Put in a serving bowl and drizzle with a little olive oil. Garnish with cilantro/coriander leaves and serve at room temperature with warmed flatbreads on the side.

tempura of mixed veggies with citrus dipping sauce

8 asparagus spears, ends trimmed

1 yellow bell pepper, cut into strips

1 red bell pepper, cut into strips

2 cups/500 ml vegetable oil

6 tablespoons cornstarch/cornflour

1 cup/125 g all-purpose/plain flour

¼ teaspoon baking powder

½ teaspoon salt

1⅓ cups/325 ml ice water

For the citrus dipping sauce:

¼ cup/65 ml Japanese soy sauce (such as Kikkoman)

1 tablespoon freshly squeezed lemon juice

1 tablespoon freshly squeezed lime juice

1 tablespoon freshly squeezed orange juice

Serves 4

Tempura is often perceived as an art form not to be attempted without a manual. This couldn't be further from the truth. Just follow a few simple rules. Use crisp vegetables without too high a water content. Ice water is essential, as it ensures the batter is light and lacy. Don't overbeat the batter—a few quick stirs with a chopstick is all that is required and any lumps will just add texture to the cooked batter.

To make the citrus dipping sauce, put all of the ingredients in a small bowl and whisk to combine. Set aside until ready to serve.

Put the prepared vegetables on a plate near to your stovetop. Put the oil in a skillet/frying pan and set over medium/high heat. Combine the cornstarch/cornflour, flour, baking powder, and salt in a bowl. Put the ice water in another chilled bowl. Working quickly, add the flour mixture to the water, stirring for just a few seconds with a chopstick or a knife, leaving the mixture lumpy-looking.

Cook the tempura in batches. Add a small handful of vegetables to the batter, letting any excess batter drip back into the bowl. Cook for 2–3 minutes, turning often with tongs so that the batter cooks evenly all over and is light golden and lacy looking. Put the tempura on some paper towels for a minute to absorb any excess oil. Reheat the oil and repeat with the remaining vegetables and batter. Serve warm with the citrus dipping sauce on the side.

mini spring rolls with chile dipping sauce

2 tablespoons safflower/sunflower oil

2 carrots, cut into matchsticks

½ cup/50 g snow peas/mangetouts, cut into matchsticks

¾ cup/50 g finely chopped shiitake mushrooms

1-inch/2.5-cm piece of fresh ginger, peeled and grated

1 small fresh red chile, seeded and chopped

1 cup/50 g bean sprouts

2 scallions/spring onions, thinly sliced

1 tablespoon light soy sauce

2 teaspoons all-purpose/plain flour

8 x 8-inch/20-cm square spring-roll wrappers

vegetable oil, for deep-frying

For the chile dipping sauce:

5 tablespoons bottled sweet chile sauce

1 tablespoon light soy sauce

Makes 16

Spring rolls are best served immediately after cooking, but to keep last-minute preparation minimal make the filling up to 24 hours ahead. Fill the wrappers about an hour before cooking, but keep them covered so they remain moist until cooked.

Heat the oil in a wok or large skillet/frying pan and stir-fry the carrots, snow peas/mangetouts, mushrooms, and ginger for 1 minute. Add the chile, bean sprouts, and scallions/spring onions and stir-fry for 1–2 minutes, or until the vegetables are tender-crisp. Remove from the heat, stir in the soy sauce and set aside to cool.

To make the chile dipping sauce, mix together the sweet chile sauce and soy sauce in a small bowl and transfer to a serving dish.

In a small bowl, mix the flour with 1 tablespoon water to make a paste. Cut the spring-roll wrappers in half diagonally and place under a damp cloth to keep moist. Remove one at a time to fill.

Divide the filling into four and put a quarter of one batch on the long cut side of a wrapper, placing it along the center, slightly in from the edge. Fold over the side flaps. Brush a little flour paste on the pointed end of the wrapper and roll up towards the point, pressing the end to seal. Repeat with the remaining wrappers. Keep covered until ready to cook.

Heat the oil in a deep, heavy-based saucepan to 400 F (200 C) or until a cube of bread burns brown in 30 seconds. Deep-fry the rolls in batches for 2–3 minutes, until crisp and golden. Drain on paper towels. Serve hot with the chile dipping sauce on the side.

sesame sweet potato wedges with peanut dipping sauce

650 g/1½ lbs. sweet potatoes, well scrubbed but unpeeled, cut lengthwise into thick wedges

2 tablespoons olive oil

1 tablespoon toasted sesame oil

1 tablespoon sesame seeds

sea salt

chopped cilantro/fresh coriander, to serve

For the peanut dipping sauce:

2 tablespoons organic crunchy peanut butter

1 tablespoon freshly squeezed lime juice

½ fresh red serrano chile, seeded and sliced

1 tablespoon soy sauce

1 tablespoon tomato ketchup

sea salt and freshly ground black pepper

Serves 6–8

If you love peanuts you'll really appreciate this dipping sauce. It works superbly with the sweetness of the potato, which can be either roasted or deep-fried. These wedges are particularly good served hot with an ice cold beer.

Preheat the oven to 400°F (200°C) Gas 6.

Arrange the sweet potato wedges in a single layer on the baking sheet, then sprinkle with the olive and sesame oils, sesame seeds, and salt. Roast in the preheated oven for about 35 minutes, or until tender (the cooking time will vary depending on the size of the wedges.)

Meanwhile, to prepare the peanut dipping sauce, put the peanut butter, lime juice, chile, soy sauce, and tomato ketchup in a food processor, add ¼ cup/65 ml hot water and blend until smooth. Season to taste with salt and pepper, then pour into a saucepan and heat gently.

Sprinkle the sweet potato wedges with the cilantro/coriander and serve with a separate bowl of the peanut dipping sauce.

ribbon vegetable and hummus chapatti wraps

2 chapatti wraps (see below)

4 tablespoons hummus (see page 62)

1 carrot

½ a red, orange, or yellow bell pepper, seeded and thinly sliced

a handful of watercress, rinsed

For the chapatti wraps:

1¼ cups/200 g whole-wheat/ wholemeal flour, stoneground if available

a pinch of sea salt

Serves 2

These simple Indian-style flat breads are delicious filled with homemade hummus (see page 62) and crisp raw vegetables. The recipe given makes six wraps but any not used can be frozen and reheated another time.

To make the chapatti wraps, stir the flour together with the salt in a mixing bowl. Gradually mix in enough cold water (7–8 tablespoons) to give a soft but not sticky dough that comes together easily. Tip the dough out onto a lightly floured surface and knead for 4–5 minutes. Shape the dough into 6 balls and rest them under the upturned bowl for 30 minutes.

Dip each ball of dough in a little flour and roll out to a 8-inch/20-cm circle. Preheat a non-stick skillet/frying pan over medium/high heat. Add one chapatti and cook for about 90 seconds, flipping over a couple of times, until the flat bread is patterned with brown spots and is cooked. Repeat with the remaining chapattis.

Use the chapattis wraps while still warm or if they have cooled, gently warm them to make them more flexible, either by dry-frying for a few seconds each side in a skillet/frying pan, or in the microwave for 10 seconds on high. Spread each one with 2 tablespoons of hummus. Use a vegetable peeler to shave the carrot into ribbons, then divide these between the wraps. Add the bell pepper slices and watercress, roll up the wraps, and cut in half to serve.

spicy bean burritos

1 red onion, sliced

1 red or yellow bell pepper, seeded and sliced

1 teaspoon safflower/sunflower oil

2 large flat mushrooms, thickly sliced

1 garlic clove, crushed

3 teaspoons Cajun spice mix or mild chili powder

2 tomatoes, chopped

14-oz./410-g can pinto beans, drained and rinsed

freshly squeezed juice of ½ a lime

4 whole-wheat/wholemeal tortillas or Chapattis (see page 57)

4 tablespoons vegan sour cream substitute (such as Tofutti) or Guacamole (see page 45)

1 cup/100 g shredded iceberg lettuce

sea salt and freshly ground black pepper

Serves 4

This is a filling and tasty lunch with a distinctly Mexican feel. If you can't find a vegan sour cream substitute, you can use guacamole (see page 45), which adds a similarly moist texture but do hold back on the Cajun spice in the recipe below as the guacamole is already hot and spicy.

Fry the onion and bell peppers in the oil for 3 minutes in a non-stick skillet/frying pan. Add the mushrooms, garlic, and 2 teaspoons of the Cajun spice mix and stir-fry for 1 minute, then mix in the tomatoes, cover the pan and cook for 2 minutes.

Meanwhile, roughly mash the beans together with the remaining Cajun spice mix and the lime juice, and season to taste with salt and pepper.

Gently warm the tortillas to refresh them and make them more flexible (see page 57), then spread each one with 1 tablespoon of vegan sour cream. Spoon on a quarter of the mashed beans and a quarter of the vegetable mixture. Top with shredded lettuce and roll up to serve.

singaras with fresh mango salsa

1 lb./450 g floury potatoes, suitable for mashing, cut into chips

8 curry leaves or 3 bay leaves

1 tablespoon vegetable oil, plus extra for deep-frying

2 onions, finely chopped

2 garlic cloves, crushed

2 hottish fresh green chiles, seeded and finely chopped

1 teaspoon ground cumin

leaves from a small bunch of cilantro/fresh coriander, chopped

16 small spring roll wrappers, cut into 2 pieces or 8 large wrappers, cut into 3 pieces

sea salt

For the fresh mango salsa:

5 pink Thai shallots or 2 regular shallots, finely chopped

finely grated zest and juice of 1 lime

½ teaspoon sugar (optional)

2 ripe mangoes, peeled and cut into small cubes

2 fresh red chiles, seeded and finely chopped

leaves from a small bunch of fresh mint, finely chopped

leaves from a small bunch of cilantro/fresh coriander, finely chopped

Serves 6–8

Singaras are a kind of Indian samosa, but they are made here with spring roll wrappers rather than heavy pastry. They are wonderful on their own, with a squeeze of lemon, or with a fruity salsa like this one.

Put the freshly cut potato chips in a saucepan of cold water, add the curry leaves, bring to a boil, then add salt. When the potatoes are soft, drain and cover with a clean kitchen towel for 5 minutes. Chop the curry leaves into the potatoes or, if using bay leaves, discard them. Put the potatoes in a bowl and set aside.

Heat the oil in a skillet/frying pan, add the onions and garlic and fry until soft and very pale golden. Mash the potatoes, then stir in the onions, garlic, chiles, cumin, and chopped cilantro/coriander. Stir briefly and let cool.

Put a strip of spring roll wrapper on a work surface and put 1 or 2 teaspoons of mixture in the bottom left hand corner, depending on the size of wrappers you are using. Fold over to the right to make a triangle. Continue folding, end to end, then wet the edge with a little water and press firmly to seal.

Heat the oil in a deep, heavy-based saucepan to 400°F (200°C) or until a cube of bread turns brown in 25 seconds. Add the singaras in batches and fry for about 2 minutes each, turning occasionally. Remove and drain on paper towels while you cook the remainder. They can be made in advance, and reheated in the oven, or served cold.

To make the salsa, put the shallots in a bowl, add the lime zest and juice, and sugar, if using, and set aside for 5 minutes. Just before serving, stir in the mangoes, chiles, mint, and cilantro/coriander. Serve with the singaras.

deep-fried yellow bean balls with Thai-style sticky sauce

1 cup/250 g dried split mung beans, soaked in water for 30 minutes and drained

1 tablespoon all-purpose/plain flour

1 teaspoon Thai red curry paste (see note on page 16)

2 tablespoons light soy sauce

2 teaspoons sugar

5 kaffir lime leaves, rolled into a cylinder and finely sliced into slivers

peanut or safflower/sunflower oil, for deep-frying

For the Thai-style sticky sauce:

4 tablespoons sugar

6 tablespoons rice vinegar

½ teaspoon sea salt

Serves 4

This so-called traditional Thai dish actually originated in India but has been adapted to suit the Thai taste by the addition of more fresh chiles. The bean balls are easy to make and delicious served hot with the sticky sauce for dipping.

To make the sauce, put the sugar, vinegar and salt in a small saucepan or wok and heat gently until the sugar dissolves. Let cool before serving with the bean balls.

To make the balls, pound the drained mung beans with a mortar and pestle or use a blender to form a coarse paste. Stirring well after each addition, add the flour, curry paste, soy sauce, sugar, and lime leaves. Pluck a small piece of the paste and form into a ball the size of a walnut. Do not mold too tightly.

Heat the oil in a deep, heavy-based saucepan to 400°F (200°C) or until a cube of bread turns brown in 25 seconds. Working in batches if necessary, add the balls and fry until golden brown. Remove with a slotted spoon, drain on paper towels, and serve hot with the sauce on the side for dipping.

stuffed vine leaves

8 oz./225 g preserved vine leaves

4 tablespoons extra-virgin olive oil

1¾ cups/450 ml hot water

For the stuffing:

freshly squeezed juice of 1 lemon, strained

1 cup/150 g long grain rice, rinsed

2 large onions, finely chopped

5 scallions/spring onions, trimmed and thinly sliced

4 tablespoons fresh dill, finely chopped

2 tablespoons finely chopped fresh mint

2 tablespoons finely chopped fresh flat-leaf parsley

5 tablespoons extra virgin olive oil

sea salt and freshly ground black pepper

Makes 50

There are many versions of stuffed vine leaves but this simple version is undoubtedly the star of the show. A good aromatic Greek olive oil is a must. They are a little time-consuming to make, but invite your friends around and enlist some help.

First wash the vine leaves and soak them in several changes of water for 1 hour.

To make the stuffing, put half the lemon juice in a large bowl. Add the rice, onions, scallions/spring onions, dill, mint, parsley, olive oil, salt, and pepper and stir well.

Line the base of a wide saucepan with 4 or 5 vine leaves. Place a vine leaf, rough side up, on a chopping board (handle the leaves carefully as they are fragile.) Put a heaping teaspoon of the stuffing near the stalk end, fold the 2 opposite sides over the stuffing, and roll up tightly like a fat cigar. Repeat with the remaining leaves.

Arrange the stuffed vine leaves in tight circles in the saucepan with the loose ends underneath. Pour the olive oil and the remaining lemon juice over the top and set a small inverted plate on top to stop them opening up while cooking. Add the hot water, cover, and simmer gently for 50 minutes.

Serve hot or at room temperature.

vegetable potstickers with orange dipping sauce

3 cups/300 g finely shredded red cabbage

1 teaspoon sea salt flakes

2 tablespoons vegetable oil, plus about ¼ cup/65 ml for shallow-frying

1 tablespoon finely grated fresh ginger

4 garlic cloves, finely chopped

1 small carrot, grated

1 tablespoon light soy sauce

18 gow gee, wonton, or gyoza wrappers

½ cup/125 ml vegetable stock

4 scallions/spring onions, thinly sliced

a handful of roughly chopped cilantro/fresh coriander

freshly ground black pepper

For the orange dipping sauce:

¼ cup/65 ml light soy sauce

¼ cup/65 ml rice vinegar

¼ cup/65 ml freshly squeezed orange juice

Makes 18

These delicious little Chinese dumplings are first pan-fried until their bottoms are crispy and golden, then stock is quickly poured over and they are steamed in the resulting hot vapour.

To make the orange dipping sauce, put all of the ingredients in a bowl and whisk to combine. Cover and set aside until ready to serve.

Put the cabbage in a bowl and sprinkle over the salt flakes. Cover and let sit for 30 minutes, stirring a few times. Put the cabbage in a colander and squeeze out as much liquid as possible. Tip it onto a chopping board and finely chop. Transfer to a bowl and set aside.

Put the 2 tablespoons oil in a large skillet/frying pan and set over high heat. Add the ginger and garlic and stir-fry for just a few seconds. Add the cabbage and carrot and stir-fry for 1 minute. Add the soy sauce and season with black pepper. Transfer to a bowl and let cool.

Put 2 teaspoons of the cabbage mixture in the center of a wrapper. Brush around the edges with a little water and bring the two sides together to form a half-moon shape, enclosing the filling. Firmly crimp around the edges to seal. Gently tap the dumplings so that they get a flattened bottom.

Cook the potstickers in 2 batches. Put half of the oil for shallow-frying in a non-stick skillet/frying pan and set over medium heat. Add the first batch of potstickers to the pan and cook for 2–3 minutes until the bottoms sizzle in the oil and turn crisp and golden. Shake the pan while they are cooking so that they don't stick. Carefully add half of the stock, be careful as it will splutter. Quickly cover with a lid and let cook for 2–3 minutes, until the filling is cooked through. Cook the second batch in the same way. Sprinkle with cilantro/coriander and scallions/spring onions and serve warm with the orange dipping sauce on the side.

falafel with avocado, tomato, and red onion salsa

1¼ cups/250 g dried chickpeas, soaked in cold water for 24 hours

2 garlic cloves, crushed

1 teaspoon ground cumin

½ teaspoon ground coriander

½ teaspoon baking soda/bicarbonate or soda

2 scallions/spring onions, very finely chopped

3 tablespoons each of chopped fresh flat-leaf parsley and cilantro/fresh coriander

sea salt and freshly ground black pepper

sunflower/safflower oil for deep-frying

pitta bread, to serve

For the avocado, tomato, and red onion salsa:

4 ripe tomatoes

1 large ripe avocado

½ red onion, finely chopped

½ small fresh red chile, halved, seeded, and very finely chopped

3 tablespoons chopped cilantro/fresh coriander

finely grated peel and juice of 1 lime

2–3 tablespoons extra-virgin olive oil

sea salt and freshly ground black pepper

Serves 4

Good falafel are light and full of flavor. It really is worthwhile using dried and soaked chickpeas—canned ones will make the mix too soft and claggy. These should be bright green with herbs, and make an ideal, protein-rich light lunch.

Soak the chickpeas in plenty of cold water. The next day, drain them very well and roll in paper towels to dry them. Transfer to a food processor, add the garlic, cumin, coriander, chili powder, and baking soda/bicarbonate of soda and blend to a smooth paste. Taste and season well with salt and pepper. Tip into a bowl, cover, and let rest for 30 minutes.

Add the scallions/spring onions, parsley, and cilantro/coriander to the chickpea paste, beat well, then knead the mixture to bring it together. Scoop out small lumps and make into flat, round cakes—as small or large as you like—and put them on a nonstick tray. Cover and chill for 15 minutes.

To make the salsa, cut the tomatoes in half, deseed them, then chop finely and put in a bowl. Chop the avocado and add to the bowl. Add the onion, chile, and cilantro/coriander and stir gently. Put the lime juice, zest, olive oil, salt, and pepper in a small bowl and mix well. Pour over the tomato mixture, fold gently and set aside.

Heat the oil in a deep, heavy-based saucepan to 375°F (190°C) or until a cube of bread turns brown in 30 seconds. Cook the falafel, in batches if necessary, for 2–3 minutes until they are crisp and brown, turning them over once. Lift out with a slotted spoon and drain on paper towels. Serve hot or warm, with pitta bread and the salsa on the side.

Indian vegetable fritters with green chutney

½ a large cucumber, cut crosswise into thick slices

½ a large cauliflower, broken into small florets

peanut or safflower/sunflower oil, for deep-frying

lemon wedges, to serve

For the batter:

2 cups/225 g chickpea flour (called *gram* flour or *besan* in Asian grocers and *farina de ceci* in Italian gourmet stores)

½ teaspoon cumin seeds

a large pinch of chili powder

1 teaspoon sea salt

For the green chutney:

2 handfuls of fresh mint leaves, finely chopped

a handful of cilantro/fresh coriander, finely chopped

2 fresh green chiles, chopped

freshly squeezed juice of ½ a lemon

a pinch of sea salt

Serves 4–6

These deep-fried snacks are popular street food in India. They can be made with most vegetables and the spices can be varied too. Mashed potatoes also work, but the spices are fried in oil first and then added to the mash rather than the batter.

To make the green chutney, put the mint, cilantro/coriander, chiles, lemon juice, and salt into a blender and blend to a purée, adding water to let the blades run. Set aside until ready to serve.

To make the batter, put the chickpea flour into a large bowl and add the spices and salt. Mix with a fork, breaking up any lumps. Add enough water (a little at a time) to make a thick, smooth batter, whisking to achieve the right consistency. The batter should be thick enough to coat and cling to the vegetables

Heat the oil in a deep, heavy-based saucepan to 375°F (190°C) or until a cube of bread turns brown in 30 seconds. Dip a cucumber slice into the batter and coat well. Using tongs, carefully slide it into the oil. Fry in batches without overcrowding the pan, for a few minutes until golden, turning them several times. As each piece is done, lift it out with a slotted spoon or tongs and drain in a colander lined with paper towels. As soon as one batch is drained, transfer the pieces to a plate and keep them warm in a low oven until all are cooked. When all the cucumber has been fried, repeat with the cauliflower, which will take slightly longer to cook.

Serve with the green chutney and lemon wedges for squeezing.

salads

pickled spring vegetable and marinated tofu salad

12 sugar snap peas

12 snowpeas/mangetouts, halved lengthwise

a bunch of asparagus, trimmed and halved crosswise

2 tablespoons white sugar

¼ cup/90 ml rice vinegar

1 small daikon (white radish), cut into julienne strips

6–8 scallions/spring onions, thinly sliced on the angle

a small bunch of cilantro/fresh coriander, chopped

3 tablespoons light soy sauce

½ teaspoon sesame oil

1 tablespoon sesame seeds, lightly toasted

For the marinated tofu:

3 tablespoons light soy sauce

½ teaspoon Chinese five-spice powder

1 lb. 5 oz./600 g firm tofu (in a block)

Serves 4

You may be able to buy dark, pressed, marinated tofu in some stores but it's easy enough to make your own at home. Its creamy texture and mildy spiced flavor goes very well with lightly-pickled spring vegetables.

To make the marinated tofu, put the soy sauce and Chinese five-spice powder in a bowl large enough to snugly fit the block of tofu. Add the tofu to the bowl and toss around to coat in the marinade. Cover with plastic wrap/clingfilm and refrigerate for a minimum of 3 hours or ideally overnight, turning often. Drain well and slice the tofu into thin batons.

Bring a saucepan of lightly salted water to a boil and add the sugar snaps, snowpeas/mangetouts, and asparagus and blanche in the hot water for 1 minute. Drain and place in a large bowl of ice water until completely cold. Drain well and put into another bowl.

Put the sugar and vinegar in small saucepan and boil for 5 minutes, until thickened slightly. Remove from the heat and let cool. Pour the vinegar mixture over the blanched vegetables and daikon, stir well and set aside or 30 minutes. Add the scallions/spring onions, cilantro/coriander, and marinated tofu to the pickled vegetables, gently tossing to combine. Mix the soy sauce and sesame oil in a small bowl and pour over the salad. Toss gently, then transfer to a serving dish and sprinkle the sesame seeds over the top. Serve immediately.

tabbouleh with chickpeas and spring salad

½ cup/90 g bulgur, fine ground if available

½ cup/125 ml boiling water

2 tablespoons freshly squeezed lemon juice

¼ cup/60 ml extra virgin olive oil

a small bunch of fresh flat-leaf parsley, finely chopped

a large handful of fresh mint leaves, finely chopped

2 tablespoons finely chopped fresh dill

about 20 cherry tomatoes, halved

14-oz./410-g can chickpeas, rinsed and drained

4 large handfuls of baby salad greens

sea salt and freshly ground black pepper

lemon wedges, to serve

toasted pitta bread or Turkish pide, to serve (optional)

Serves 4

Bulgur it often confused with cracked wheat but it is not exactly the same thing. The wheat kernels have been steamed, dried, and crushed to give a tender, chewy texture which is excellent for pilafs and wholesome salads, such as tabbouleh.

Put the bulgur in a heatproof bowl and pour over the boiling water. Stir once, cover tightly with plastic wrap/clingfilm, and set aside for 8–10 minutes. Put the lemon juice and olive oil in a small bowl and whisk. Pour over the bulgur and stir well with a fork, fluffing up the bulgur and separating the grains.

Put the bulgur in a large bowl with the parsley, mint, dill, tomatoes, chickpeas, and salad greens. Toss everything together. Season well with salt and pepper. Transfer to serving plates and add a wedge of lemon for squeezing. Serve with toasted pitta bread or Turkish pide, if liked.

cashew salad with tamarind dressing

8 Chinese leaves (Chinese or Napa cabbage)

1 large carrot

1 cucumber, about halved, seeded, cut into 2-inch/5-cm sections, then finely sliced lengthwise

6 scallions/spring onions, sliced diagonally

8 slices dried mango, chopped

½ cup/75 g cashews, toasted in a dry skillet/frying pan and coarsely crushed

For the tamarind dressing:

2 oz./50 g tamarind pulp or 1½ tablespoons tamarind paste*

½ teaspoon Szechuan peppercorns, lightly toasted in a dry skillet/frying pan and coarsely crushed

2 teaspoons sesame oil

1 garlic clove, finely chopped

½ teaspoon brown sugar or jaggery (palm sugar), to taste

2 tablespoons chopped Thai basil, Vietnamese mint, or cilantro/fresh coriander

sea salt, to taste

Serves 4

This fragant salad is full of South-east Asian flavors but also with a hint of Chinese. Tamarind and Szechuan pepper form an unusual partnership in the dressing but the combination of sour and hot is delicious so do give it a try.

To make the tamarind water for the dressing, put the tamarind pulp in a small glass bowl. Add 1 cup/250 ml warm water and let it soak for 15 minutes. Then squeeze the tamarind through your fingers in the water and continue until all of it has been squeezed into a pulp. Press through a strainer/sieve. (If using tamarind paste, omit this stage.)

Put 6 tablespoons of the strained tamarind water, the Szechuan pepper, sesame oil, garlic, sugar, and chopped herbs into a screw-top jar and shake well. Set aside.

Stack the Chinese leaves on top of each other and slice them finely. Grate the carrot into long sticks using the large blade of a box grater, or slice finely into long strips. Divide the shredded leaves between serving plates, add a layer of grated carrot, then the cucumber strips. Top with the scallions/spring onions, and dried mango. Drizzle the dressing over the salad, top with the cashews, then serve immediately.

*Note: Tamarind lends a rich, sweet-sour flavor to dishes. The tropical trees produce fresh pods that are either sold fresh or processed into pulp or paste for convenience and long shelf life. Look out for it in Asian or Caribbean grocers—semi-dried tamarind pulp (also known as "lump" tamarind) comes in soft rectangular blocks sealed in plastic wrap. The darker concentrated paste is sold in tubs and is a more processed product.

couscous salad with artichokes and harissa dressing

½ cup/90 g couscous

1 cup/250 ml hot vegetable stock

12 sun-blushed (semi-dried) tomatoes or 12 fresh cherry tomatoes, halved

4 marinated artichoke hearts, sliced

4 scallions/spring onions, sliced

2 x 14-oz./410-g cans chickpeas, rinsed and drained

a handful of fresh flat-leaf parsley, coarsely chopped, plus a few extra sprigs to garnish

a few sprigs of watercress

For the harissa dressing:

⅓ cup/85 ml tablespoons extra virgin olive oil

2 tablespoons sherry vinegar or cider vinegar

2 tablespoon harissa paste*

sea salt and freshly ground black pepper

Serves 4

This quick and easy salad is endlessly adaptable so do feel free to experiment with different vegetables and fresh herbs. Easy-cook couscous is usually just soaked then drained, but if you steam it after soaking you get a lighter, fluffy result.

Put the couscous in a heatproof bowl and pour in the hot stock. Leave for 15 minutes until the water has been absorbed. For a fluffier texture, put the soaked couscous in a strainer/sieve and steam over a pan of simmering water for another 10 minutes. Fluff up with a fork and set aside to cool.

To make the harissa dressing, put the olive oil, vinegar, and harissa paste in a bowl and beat with a fork. Season to taste with salt and pepper.

When ready to make up the salad, tip the couscous in a large bowl, stir in the tomatoes, artichoke hearts, scallions/spring onions, chickpeas, and parsley. Sprinkle half the dressing over the couscous mixture and toss with a fork. Add the watercress and parsley sprigs and serve. Serve the extra dressing separately for people to help themselves.

*Note: Harissa is a fiercely hot red chile paste from North Africa, where it is used extensively as a condiment and diluted with stock, water, or fresh tomato sauce to flavor couscous dishes, soups, and tagines (stews.) Moroccan food is growing in popularity so harissa paste is now widely available in larger supermarkets and from specialist online retailers.

fennel and orange salad

5 large oranges, about 1½ lbs./600 g, or equivalent weight of clementines, satsumas, or mandarins, washed and dried

1–2 heads of young fennel, preferably with green tops

2 red onions, thinly sliced

24 black olives, preferably the dry-cured Provençal type

For the dressing:

4 tablespoons extra-virgin olive oil

½ teaspoon orange flower water or 1 tablespoon fresh orange juice

1 teaspoon sea salt

½ teaspoon white, green or pink peppercorns, well crushed

Serves 4

This Arab-influenced salad uses young, tender fennel bulbs, and choose juicy oranges. To cut off all of the bitter pith, slice a piece off the top and base of each fruit, then slice off the skin and white pith from top to bottom using a fine, serrated knife, in a sawing movement—easy and effective. Orange flower water is sold in Italian and Middle Eastern shops.

Using a vegetable peeler, remove the peel of 1 orange (or 2 smaller citrus fruits), then slice the peel into thin strips. Alternatively use a zester or canelle knife. Set aside. Halve and squeeze the juice from the fruit into a bowl.

Remove a slice from the top and bottom of the remaining fruit then prepare as described in the recipe introduction. Discard the debris. Slice each fruit crosswise into thin rounds, adding any juice to the bowl.

Finely slice the fennel bulb lengthwise. Toss it immediately in the bowl of juice. Assemble the fennel, oranges, onions, and olives on serving plates, then add the reserved peel and pour the juice over the top.

To make the dressing, put the olive oil, orange flower water, salt, and pepper in a bowl and whisk well with a fork. Pour the dressing over the salad and serve immediately.

Provençal pickled beans

4 oz./115 g tiny pickling onions or other pearl onions

12 oz./350 g green beans and/or wax beans, stemmed

1 oz./25 g currants

lemon wedges, to serve

For the wine dressing:

freshly squeezed juice of ½ a lemon

6 tablespoons extra-virgin olive oil

2 tablespoons sweet wine, such as Muscat

1 tablespoon balsamic vinegar or red wine vinegar

2 teaspoons pomegranate molasses, plus extra to serve (see note on page 34)

1 fresh green chile, thinly sliced

1 teaspoon coriander seeds, lightly crushed

sea salt and freshly ground black pepper

Serves 4

The green bean salad, especially served warm, is a classic French dish with many variations. In this recipe, the vinaigrette combines sweet wine and lightly crushed coriander seeds with delicious results.

Put the onions, beans, and currants in a saucepan, add a pinch of salt and cover with boiling water. Simmer until the onions are barely soft and the beans are bright green and snap-tender. Drain, refresh in cold water and pat dry.

Put the lemon juice, oil, wine, vinegar, pomegranate molasses, chile, and coriander seeds in a bowl and whisk well with a fork. Season to taste with salt and pepper. Pour the dressing over the vegetables.

Drizzle extra pomegranate molasses over the top and add a lemon wedge to each plate. Serve immediately.

Tuscan panzanella

6 very ripe tomatoes

2 garlic cloves, sliced into slivers

4 thick slices day-old bread, preferably Italian-style, such as ciabatta

about 4 inches/10 cm cucumber, halved, seeded, and thinly sliced

1 red onion, finely chopped

1 tablespoon chopped fresh flat-leaf parsley

8–12 tablespoons extra virgin olive oil

2 tablespoons white wine vinegar, cider vinegar, or sherry vinegar

1 teaspoon balsamic vinegar

leaves from a small bunch of fresh flat-leaf parsley or basil, roughly torn

12 caperberries or 4 tablespoons salted capers, rinsed and drained

sea salt and freshly ground black pepper

a ridged, stovetop grill pan, lightly brushed with oil

Serves 4

There are many variations of this Tuscan bread salad. The trick is to let the flavors blend well without allowing the bread to disintegrate into a mush. Always use the ripest and reddest tomatoes you can find—you could use one of the full-flavored heirloom varieties, or at least an Italian plum tomato.

Preheat the oven to 350°F (180°C) Gas 4. Cut the tomatoes in half, spike with slivers of garlic, and roast in the preheated oven for about 1 hour, or until wilted and some of the moisture has evaporated.

Meanwhile, put the bread on the prepared grill pan and cook until lightly toasted and barred with grill marks on both sides. Tear or cut the toast into pieces and put into a salad bowl. Sprinkle with a little water until damp.

Add the tomatoes, cucumber, onion, parsley, salt, and pepper. Drizzle with the olive oil and vinegars, toss well, then set aside for about 1 hour to let the flavors develop.

When ready to serve, add the parsley or basil and caperberries, toss and serve immediately.

saffron potato salad with sun-dried tomatoes and basil dressing

1 lb./450 g large waxy yellow-fleshed potatoes, peeled

a pinch of saffron threads, about 20

8 sun-dried tomatoes (the dry kind, not in oil)

For the basil dressing:

6 tablespoons extra virgin olive oil

3 tablespoons chopped fresh basil leaves, plus extra to serve

2 tablespoons salted capers, rinsed, drained and chopped if large

1–2 tablespoons freshly squeezed lemon juice

sea salt and freshly ground black pepper

Serves 4

In this recipe, the potatoes absorb the glorious golden color and subtle flavor of the saffron as they simmer gently with the tomatoes. So serve this salad warm, as the heat will release the heady aromas of the basil and saffron.

Cut the potatoes into large chunks. Put them in a saucepan, add enough cold water to just cover them, then add the saffron and sun-dried tomatoes. Bring slowly to a boil, then turn down the heat, cover, and simmer very gently for about 12 minutes until just tender. (If the water boils too fast, the potatoes will start to disintegrate.) Drain well.

Pick out the now plumped up sun-dried tomatoes and slice them thinly. Tip the potatoes into a large bowl and add the sliced tomatoes.

To make the basil dressing, put the oil, basil, and capers in a small bowl and whisk with a fork. Season to taste with lemon juice, salt, and pepper and mix well. Pour over the hot potato mixture, mix gently, then serve hot or warm, scattered with extra basil leaves.

grilled eggplant with salmoriglio dressing

2 medium eggplants/aubergines, thinly sliced

2 tablespoons extra virgin olive oil

sea salt

For the salmoriglio dressing:

2 tablespoons red wine vinegar

1–2 teaspoons sugar

finely grated peel/zest and juice of ½ a lemon

4 tablespoons extra virgin olive oil

1 garlic clove, finely chopped

2 tablespoons fresh mint leaves, finely chopped, plus extra leaves to serve

1 tablespoon salted capers, rinsed, drained, and chopped if large

a ridged, stovetop grill pan, brushed with oil (optional)

Serves 4

This is a delicious salad. Make it in large quantities and keep it in the fridge for a quick snack—the eggplant/aubergine just gets better as it absorbs the lemony dressing. It can be eaten on it's own or served as part of a mixed vegetable antipasto.

To make the salmoriglio dressing, put the vinegar and sugar in a bowl and stir until dissolved. Add the grated lemon peel, juice, and oil and whisk well. Stir in the garlic, chopped mint, and capers and set aside to infuse.

Meanwhile, spread out the eggplant/aubergine slices in a colander and sprinkle with salt. Let drain for 20 minutes. Rinse well, pat dry with paper towels, then brush the slices with olive oil.

Heat the grill pan until smoking. Alternatively, preheat a conventional broiler/grill to high. Grill the eggplant/aubergine slices in batches for 2–3 minutes on each side until golden brown and lightly charred. Arrange the slices on a large plate and spoon the dressing over the top. Cover and set aside for 30 minutes so the eggplants/aubergines absorb the dressing. Sprinkle with extra mint leaves and serve.

nutty rice salad with preserved lemon dressing

½ cup/100 g wild rice

½ cup/100 g brown basmati rice

½ cup/100 g white long-grain rice

½ cup/75 g currants, soaked in warm water for 10 minutes, then drained

½ cup/75 g dried cherries, chopped if large

1 large bulb of fennel, trimmed and chopped, feathery tops reserved

1 teaspoon cumin seeds, crushed

a bunch of scallions/spring onions, thinly sliced

⅓ cup/50 g blanched slivered/flaked almonds, toasted

⅓ cup/50 g shelled pistachios, chopped

3 tablespoons chopped cilantro/ fresh coriander

freshly ground black pepper

cos lettuce leaves, to serve

For the preserved lemon dressing:

5 tablespoons extra virgin olive oil

1–2 tablespoons freshly squeezed lemon juice

1 garlic clove, crushed

2 tablespoons chopped preserved lemons*

½–1 teaspoon sugar, to taste

Serves 6–8

The essential ingredient in this deliciously nutty rice salad is the preserved lemons in the dressing—they add a lovely mellow yet sharp flavor.

Cook each variety of rice in a separate saucepan of boiling water over medium heat until tender. The wild rice takes up to 40 minutes, brown rice about 25 minutes, and long-grain rice should be tender in 15 minutes. Drain the rice into a colander. Rinse briefly with hot water, then leave to drain well, fluffing up with a fork after 5 minutes.

Meanwhile, make the preserved lemon dressing. Put the oil and the lemon juice in a bowl, whisk well, then stir in the garlic and preserved lemon. Season to taste with pepper and sugar. Toss the cooked rice with half the dressing, the currants, and the cherries.

Heat the remaining oil in a skillet/frying pan and cook the fennel and cumin seeds gently for 5 minutes until softened but not browned. Add the onions and cook for another 1–2 minutes. Stir into the rice with the nuts, cilantro/coriander, and chopped fennel tops. Let the salad sit for 30 minutes, then stir in the remaining dressing and serve with the lettuce.

*Note: Preserved lemons are used extensively in North African cooking and are whole lemons packed in jars with salt. The interesting thing is that you eat only the peel, which contains the essential flavor of the lemon. They are available from some larger supermarkets and specialist online retailers.

cauliflower and Swiss chard salad

¼ cup/65 ml light olive oil

1 small head of cauliflower, separated into large florets

1 teaspoon ground cumin

6 large Swiss chard leaves, cut into strips

1 red onion, cut into wedges

2 garlic cloves, chopped

14-oz./400-g can chickpeas, rinsed and drained

¼ cup/65 ml tahini

2 tablespoons freshly squeezed lemon juice

¼ teaspoon white pepper

sea salt

Serves 4

Cauliflower is so often overlooked in favor of other brassicas, such as broccoli, that are quicker to cook. It's a shame as it has a pleasingly firm texture and works well in soups and curries or, as here, in a spicy Middle Eastern-style salad.

Put the oil in a skillet/frying pan set over high heat, add the cauliflower florets and cook for 8–10 minutes, turning often, until they are a dark, golden brown. Add the cumin and cook, stirring, for 1 minute. Add the Swiss chard, onion, and garlic to the pan and cook for 2–3 minutes. Add the chickpeas and stir. Season to taste with salt.

Combine the tahini, lemon juice, and white pepper in a small bowl and add a little salt to taste. Whisk to combine. Transfer the vegetables to a bowl and drizzle the dressing over the top to serve.

Turkish mint and parsley salad

½ cup/90 g bulgur

2 tomatoes, halved, seeded, and chopped, with the juices reserved

1 red onion or shallot, finely chopped and soaked in a little lemon juice

½ cucumber, peeled in strips, seeded, and cut into cubes

2 tablespoons extra virgin olive oil

a pinch of cayenne pepper

1 teaspoon ground sumac*
or the freshly squeezed juice of
½ a lemon

leaves from a bunch of fresh flat-leaf parsley, coarsely chopped

leaves from a bunch of fresh mint, coarsely chopped

sea salt and freshly ground
black pepper

lemon and lime wedges, to serve

Serves 2–4

This Turkish dish of bulgur wheat and herbs (kisir) is similar to the more familiar Lebanese tabbouleh. Traditionally, this salad is served with pickled vegetables on boiled vine leaves but it can be served simply with lemon and lime wedges.

Put the bulgur in a bowl and cover with ⅔ cup/150 ml cold water. Let stand for about 40 minutes to absorb the liquid.

Put the bulgur in a strainer/sieve and squeeze out any excess water. Transfer to a serving bowl, then add the tomatoes and their juices, onion, cucumber, olive oil, cayenne, salt and pepper, and half the sumac.

Add the parsley and mint leaves to the salad, toss gently, and sprinkle with the remaining sumac. Serve with lemon and lime wedges on the side for squeezing.

*Note: Sumac is an increasingly popular spice. It grows wild, but is also cultivated in Italy, Sicily, and throughout the Middle East. It is widely used in Lebanese, Syrian, Turkish, and Iranian cooking. The red berries have an astringent quality, with a pleasing sour-fruit flavor. They are used whole, but ground sumac is available from Middle Eastern grocers or specialist online retailers.

Greek horta salad with roast beets

a large handful of beet leaves or,
if unavailable, spinach, silver beet,
Swiss chard, or ruby chard

a bunch of baby beets, about 6–8,
well washed

4 tablespoons extra virgin olive oil

1 lemon, quartered or cut into wedges

sea salt and freshly cracked
black pepper

Serves 4

**This traditional Greek salad of wilted greens dressed with
lemon juice and good olive oil can also good made with
spinach, silver beet, or ruby chard. This recipe also includes
some baby beets to make it a more substantial dish.**

Preheat the oven to 200°C (400°F) Gas 6.

Rub the beets with olive oil, sprinkle with salt, and cook in the preheated
oven for about 20–30 minutes—the cooking time will vary according to their
size so test one with a skewer after 20 minutes. When tender, remove from
the oven and let cool.

Wash the beet leaves, then put in a large saucepan just with the water
clinging to the leaves. Bring to a boil, put the lid on tightly, lower the heat
and simmer for a few minutes until the leaves are just wilted. Remove from
the heat, cool under running water, and drain. Chill until ready to serve.

When ready to serve, put the wilted beet leaves on serving plates and
drizzle with olive oil, then sprinkle with sea salt and cracked black pepper.
Arrange the roast beets on top. Serve with the lemon wedges, which should
be squeezed over just before eating.

red salad with beet and cabbage

1 quantity Harissa Dressing (see page 80)

6–8 baby beets

2–4 small whole heads of garlic, preferably pink spring garlic

olive oil, for roasting

1 small red cabbage

2 tablespoons white wine vinegar or cider vinegar

2 red onions

sea salt and freshly ground black pepper

Serves 4–6

Crushing the red cabbage and vinegar together with your hands has a miraculous effect on the cabbage, releasing its juices to make a delicious variation on regular coleslaw.

Preheat the oven to 400°F (200°C) Gas 6.

Leave the beets whole and unpeeled. Cut the top off each garlic, about ½ inch/1 cm from the stalk. You will be able to see all the cloves. Put the beets and garlic in an ovenproof dish, drizzle with olive oil, toss to coat on all sides, then sprinkle with salt and pepper. Put more oil into the garlic. Roast in the preheated oven for about 30–45 minutes, or until the beets and garlic are tender (you may have to remove the beets first.) Baste several times during cooking, spooning the oil into the garlic. When cooked, remove from the oven, let cool slightly then cut the beets into wedges.

About 15 minutes before the beets are cooked, cut the cabbage in quarters and remove the white cores. Cut the quarters into thin slices and put in a bowl. Sprinkle with vinegar and turn and mash the cabbage with your hands so the fibers break down a little and absorb it.

Cut the red onions into fine wedges, put in a bowl and cover with boiling water. Drain just before using.

When ready to serve, pop the roasted pulp out of 4 garlic cloves and put in a serving bowl. Add the harissa dressing and beat with a fork. Drain the onions, pat dry with paper towels, then add to the bowl. Add the cabbage and beets and toss gently. Season to taste with salt and pepper. Serve the remaining heads of garlic on the side for people to press out the delicious flesh themselves.

Indian potato salad

½ cup/125 ml peanut oil

1 tablespoon mustard seeds

½ tablespoon cumin seeds

½ cinnamon stick, crushed

1 dried red chile, crushed

6 cardamom pods, crushed

1 teaspoon turmeric

1 lb./450 g potatoes, cut into chunks

2 red onions, chopped

1 garlic clove, crushed

a handful of cilantro/fresh coriander, roughly torn

sea salt and freshly ground black pepper

limes wedges, to serve

Serves 4

This Indian version of a potato salad is spicy, crunchy, and wonderfully interesting. Add extra lime juice to taste. The spice mixes may be changed to suit your taste.

Put half of the oil in a saucepan, add the mustard and cumin seeds, cinnamon, chile, and cardamom. Stir-fry until aromatic, then stir in the turmeric. Add the potatoes, and a little salt and pepper and stir-fry for about 2 minutes. Add 1 cup/250 ml hot water and bring to a boil. Cook until the liquid has evaporated and the potatoes are tender—adding more water if necessary.

Sprinkle half the chopped red onion over the top of the potatoes. Put the remaining oil in a skillet/frying pan, add the remaining onion and the garlic and fry until golden brown.

Pour the contents of the skillet, including the oil, over the potatoes and toss to coat. Top with the torn cilantro/coriander and serve. Squeeze fresh lime juice over the salad to taste.

Japanese tofu salad
with sesame seeds

2 blocks silken tofu, well chilled

For the dashi*:
1 cup/100 g dried shiitake
mushrooms, coarsely chopped
1 oz./25 g dried kelp

For the dipping sauce:
4 tablespoons soy sauce
ideally wheat-free tamari
1 tablespoon sugar
4 tablespoons sake
1 cup/250 ml dashi (see above)

To serve:
2 tablespoons white sesame seeds,
lightly toasted in a dry skillet/frying pan
2 scallions/spring onions, finely sliced
2-inch/5-cm piece of fresh ginger,
peeled and finely grated

Serves 6

This elegant, simple recipe is made with silken tofu, a name that describes its texture. It should be eaten very fresh, and if you bring it home in a carton with water, drain off the water and cover with fresh cold water.

First make the dashi. Put 3½ cups/875 ml water in a large saucepan and add the shiitake mushrooms. Bring to a boil then reduce the heat and simmer for 45 minutes. Add another ½ cup/125 ml water and the kelp and bring to a boil. Remove from the heat. Pour the mixture through a colander set over a bowl. Reserve the mushrooms for another use and discard the kelp. Unused dashi will keep in an airtight container in the refrigerator for 1 week.

Put the dipping sauce ingredients into a small saucepan and heat slowly until the sugar has dissolved. Cool and chill.

Put the tofu blocks carefully on a flat plate and invert another plate over them. Put a weight, such as a can of beans, on top and set aside for at least 30 minutes. Set it on a tilt on the draining board to drain out some of the moisture. Keep cold.

To serve, cut each block of tofu into 9 cubes. Put 3 cubes in each serving bowl. Serve a small bowl of toasted sesame seeds, scallion/spring onion, and grated ginger, and another bowl with the dipping sauce to each person.

*Note: Dashi is a soup stock that is used extensively in Japanese cuisine. Traditionally, the stock is made with bonito (fish flakes) so use the vegan recipe given here to impart a similarly robust flavor. If you are in a pinch for time, substitute commercial mushroom broth (such as Pacific Natural Foods Organic Mushroom Broth) for the dashi.

black rice salad with chile greens

1¼ cups/250 g Asian black rice

a handful of asparagus, halved

a handful of sugar snap peas

a handful of green beans, halved

1 cup/100 g fava/broad beans, boiled and skinned

1 fresh red chile, seeded and chopped

4 scallions/spring onions, sliced

chopped flesh of 1 lime

For the Asian dressing:

2 stalks of lemongrass, outer leaves discarded, remainder very finely chopped

1-inch/3-cm piece of fresh ginger, peeled, grated, and juice squeezed

1 fresh green chile, halved, seeded, and finely chopped

freshly squeezed juice of 1 lime

½ cup/125 ml vegetarian "fish" sauce*

2 tablespoons brown sugar

For the sushi vinegar:

⅔ cup/140 ml Japanese rice vinegar

⅓ cup/5 tablespoons sugar

4 teaspoons sea salt

2-inch/5-cm piece of fresh ginger, peeled, grated, and squeezed

3 garlic cloves, crushed

Serves 4

There are various kinds of Asian rice and most, except very sticky rice, work well in salads. This delicious recipe uses black rice but if you can't find it, use wild rice instead.

To make the Asian dressing, put all the ingredients in a saucepan, bring to a boil and simmer until the sugar has dissolved. Let cool. To make the sushi vinegar, put all the ingredients in a saucepan and simmer over low heat.

Put the rice into a large saucepan, cover with water to 1 inch/3 cm above the top of the rice and bring to a boil. Cover tightly with a lid, reduce the heat and simmer for 14 minutes. Turn off the heat, do not remove the lid, and set aside for 12 minutes. Remove the lid. The rice should be perfectly fluffy. If not, put the lid back on and boil hard for about 1 minute. Remove from the heat, drain, then run it under cold water. Drain again. Transfer to a bowl, sprinkle with the sushi vinegar and stir it through gently with a spoon.

Put the asparagus stalk ends in a saucepan of boiling salted water for 1–2 minutes or until you can just pierce them with a fork. Drain in a colander under cold running water. Add the asparagus tips and sugar snaps and cook for about 30 seconds, until just tender. Drain under cold running water. Cook the green beans and fava/broad beans, in the same way. Put all the greens in a bowl, add the chopped chile, scallions/spring onions, and lime flesh and mix well. Add the chile greens to the rice and sprinkle with the dressing. Stir gently, then serve as soon as possible.

Note: Vegetarian "fish" sauce is usually made from soy beans, salt, sugar, water, chile, and citric acid as a preservative (since it's not fermented.) Vietnamese grocers tend to carry it and some will order it for you if you ask. If you can't find it, use a light soy sauce as a substitute.

herb, red onion, and quinoa salad with preserved lemon

1 cup/150 g quinoa

1 small red onion

1 preserved lemon, finely chopped, or finely grated peel of 1 fresh lemon

3 oz./75 g arugula/rocket

leaves from a large bunch of flat-leaf parsley

leaves from a small bunch of fresh mint, chopped

a handful of chives, chopped

freshly squeezed juice of 1 lemon

¼ teaspoon ground cinnamon

4 tablespoons extra virgin olive oil

¼ teaspoon sea salt

¼ teaspoon freshly ground black pepper

Serves 6

This refreshing salad is packed with fresh green herbs and has a light touch of spice. Preserved lemons are used extensively in North African cooking. They have an intense flavor and can really lift a dish.

Bring a medium saucepan of salted water to a boil. Rinse the quinoa in a strainer/sieve under cold running water, then add to the boiling water. Cook for 12–15 minutes until tender. Drain and let cool.

Slice the onion very finely, using a mandoline if you have one. Put in a bowl of ice water for 10 minutes. Drain well.

In a bowl, combine the quinoa, onion, preserved lemon, arugula/rocket, parsley, mint, and chives.

In a small bowl, whisk together the lemon juice, cinnamon, and add the salt and pepper. Whisk in the olive oil.

Toss the salad and dressing together just before serving.

green bean and chickpea salad with sesame dressing

1 lb./450 g green beans

2 tablespoons sake or dry sherry

3 teaspoons sugar

5 teaspoons Japanese soy sauce (such as Kikkoman)

1 cup/250 ml vegetable stock

3 tablespoons sesame seeds

14-oz/410-g can chickpeas, drained and rinsed

½ teaspoon sesame oil

Serves 6

This Japanese-inspired salad involves cooking the beans twice. The first cooking allows the green of the beans to be set as well as cooking the beans evenly while still retaining a crunch. The second gives the beans more depth of flavor.

Bring a saucepan of water to a boil, add the beans and cook for 5 minutes until bright green and tender but still firm to the bite. Drain and rinse in cold water, then plunge into ice water to set their color.

Bring the sake to a boil in a small saucepan and then transfer to a bowl and combine with the sugar and soy sauce.

Put the stock in a saucepan with 1 tablespoon of the sake mixture. Bring to a boil. Drain the beans and add to the stock. Return to a boil, then remove from the heat, drain, and let cool.

Heat a skillet/frying pan until hot, add the sesame seeds and toast, tossing them in the pan constantly, until they are golden. Transfer the toasted seeds to a mortar and pestle, mini food processor, or spice grinder and grind them to a rough paste.

In a bowl, combine the ground sesame seeds with the chickpeas, sesame oil, and the remaining sake mixture, then toss through the drained beans. Serve immediately.

tomato, avocado, and lime salad with crisp tortillas

freshly squeezed juice of 1 lime, plus 1 lime

4 ripe, firm avocados

leaves from a large bunch of cilantro/fresh coriander

24 cherry tomatoes, halved

6 tablespoons olive or avocado oil

2 garlic cloves, crushed

2 flour tortillas

sea salt and freshly ground black pepper

Serves 6

This is a good way to make the most of avocados. It makes a tasty and refreshing addition to any spicy Mexican-style bean dish.

Put the lime juice in a bowl. Cut the avocados in half, remove the pits and peel. Cut each half into 4 wedges and toss with the lime juice.

Using a small paring knife, cut the top and bottom off of the lime. Cut away the skin and pith. Carefully slice between each segment and remove the flesh. Combine the lime flesh with the avocados, cilantro/coriander, tomatoes, and 4 tablespoons of the olive oil. Season to taste with salt and pepper and set aside. Heat the broiler/grill.

In a small bowl, combine the garlic and remaining 2 tablespoons of olive oil. Brush the oil and garlic mixture over the tortillas and toast them under the preheated broiler/grill for about 1 minute until brown. (Watch them carefully as they will toast very quickly and may burn.)

Break the tortillas into pieces and scatter over the salad just before serving.

rice noodle salad with Chinese five-spice dressing

7 oz./200 g rice stick noodles

1 tablespoon groundnut oil

3 carrots, peeled

7 oz./200 g Savoy or Chinese cabbage, very thinly sliced

6 radishes, thinly sliced

3 scallions/spring onions, thinly sliced lengthwise

4 oz./100 g water chestnuts, thinly sliced

¼ cup/70 g cashew nuts or almonds, toasted and roughly chopped

For the Chinese five-spice dressing:

1 tablespoon sugar

½ teaspoon crushed fresh red chile

½ teaspoon Chinese five-spice powder

2 tablespoons Japanese soy sauce (such as Kikkoman)

2 tablespoons rice vinegar

1 tablespoon freshly squeezed lime or lemon juice

1 teaspoon sesame oil

Serves 6

This is a spicy twist on coleslaw. To turn it into a more substantial meal, simply toss through fried marinated tofu.

Put the rice stick noodles in a heatproof bowl and cover with boiling water. Leave for 5 minutes or until soft, then drain well. Toss with the groundnut oil to stop the noodles sticking together.

To make the Chinese five-spice dressing, combine the sugar, chile, five-spice powder, soy sauce, vinegar, lime juice, and sesame oil in a small bowl. Stir until the sugar has dissolved.

Cut the carrots into thin ribbons—this can be done using a mandoline if you have one, or a vegetable peeler. Put in a large bowl with the noodles, cabbage, radishes, scallions/spring onions, and water chestnuts. Add the dressing and toss to mix.

Transfer to a serving dish and scatter with the toasted nuts to serve.

roasted tomato and
red bell pepper fattoush

8 tomatoes

2 red bell peppers, halved and seeded

6 tablespoons olive oil

3 tablespoons fresh oregano or
marjoram leaves

2 large pitta breads

1 small red onion, sliced

½ cucumber, chopped

a large bunch of fresh flat-leaf parsley,
roughly chopped

a small bunch of fresh mint, roughly
chopped

freshly squeezed juice of 1 lemon

sea salt and freshly ground
black pepper

Serves 6

Fattoush is a traditional Middle Eastern salad that showcases the juicy ripeness of the tomato harvest. Roasting tomatoes condenses their flavor, but if you are lucky enough to have particularly tasty tomatoes, you can leave them raw.

Preheat the oven to 300°F (150°C) Gas 2.

Cut the tomatoes in half and scoop out the seeds. Put the seeded tomatoes and bell peppers cut-side up on a baking sheet. Drizzle with 2 tablespoons of the oil, add a little salt and pepper and sprinkle the oregano leaves over the top. Bake in the preheated oven for 1 hour. Let cool and then slice the roasted bell peppers into strips.

Raise the oven temperature to 400°F (200°C) Gas 6.

Carefully split the pitta breads in half through the middle and place rough-side up on a baking sheet. Bake in the preheated oven for 10 minutes until crisp. Let cool on a wire rack.

In a serving bowl, combine the roasted bell peppers and tomatoes, onion, cucumber, parsley, and mint. Toss through the lemon juice and 2 tablespoons of the oil and season with salt and pepper. Break the baked pitta breads into pieces and scatter these over the salad. Drizzle with the remaining oil to serve.

five-bean salad with lemon and poppy seed dressing

14-oz./410-g can white beans (butter or cannellini), drained and rinsed

14-oz./410-g can borlotti beans, drained and rinsed

10 oz./300 g green beans, trimmed

3 oz./85 g small fresh or 5 oz./150 g frozen fava/broad beans

½ cup/120 g beansprouts

For the lemon and poppy seed dressing:

3 tablespoons poppy seeds

1 small red onion

1 tablespoon maple syrup or agave nectar

1 teaspoon finely grated lemon peel

1 teaspoon sea salt flakes

¼ teaspoon freshly ground black pepper

2 tablespoons freshly squeezed lemon juice

4 tablespoons olive oil, lemon-infused if available

Serves 6

This is a more dramatic take on the old-style bean salad. The lemon and poppy seed dressing works well with any green salad or potato salad and is delicious drizzled over a platter of grilled mixed vegetables.

To make the lemon and poppy seed dressing, heat a skillet/frying pan over medium heat and add the poppy seeds. Cook, tossing in the pan, for 3 minutes until toasted. Let cool.

Grate the onion and put in a bowl with the toasted poppy seeds, syrup, lemon zest, salt, and pepper. Whisk in the lemon juice and then the oil.

In a large bowl, combine the drained cannellini and borlotti beans. Pour over the lemon and poppy seed dressing and toss well. Set aside while you prepare the other beans.

Bring a saucepan of water to a boil. Add the green beans and boil for 5 minutes until just tender. Drain and refresh in plenty of ice water.

Bring another saucepan of water to a boil. Add the fava/broad beans and boil for 2 minutes until just blanched. Drain and refresh in plenty of ice water. If using frozen beans, peel off the tough outer layer and discard.

Pour boiling water over the beansprouts to blanch, then refresh in plenty of ice water.

Drain the green beans, fava/broad beans, and beansprouts well. Add to the dressed beans and toss well before serving.

brown rice, hazelnut, and herb salad with kaffir lime dressing

1 cup/200 g brown rice

1 cup/140 g blanched hazelnuts

4 scallions/spring onions, thinly sliced

leaves from a large bunch of fresh mint

leaves from a large bunch of fresh basil, Thai basil if available

leaves from a large bunch of cilantro/fresh coriander

2 teaspoons sesame oil

edible flower petals (optional)

For the kaffir lime dressing:

1 tablespoon sugar, preferably palm sugar (jaggery), chopped

2 tablespoons rice vinegar

1 tablespoon Japanese soy sauce (sauce as Kikkoman)

1 tablespoon freshly squeezed lime juice

1 tablespoon vegetarian "fish" sauce (see note on page 107)

2 kaffir lime leaves, tough stems removed, very finely shredded

Serves 6

Rice salads are a perennial favorite. This deliciously nutty version has a hint of South-east Asian flavor. Cook the rice on the day you are making the salad, as it will go hard and unpleasant if refrigerated for too long.

To make the kaffir lime dressing, gently heat the sugar and vinegar together in a small saucepan, stirring until the sugar has dissolved. Let cool, then combine with the soy sauce, lime juice, vegetarian "fish" sauce, and kaffir lime leaves. Set aside until needed.

Bring 2 cups/500 ml water to a boil, add ½ teaspoon salt and the rice and bring back to a boil. Stir, cover, lower the heat to very low and cook undisturbed for 25 minutes. Turn off the heat, let rest for 5 minutes, then stir with a fork to fluff up (drain off excess water if necessary.) Put in a serving bowl, toss with the dressing, and leave to cool.

Preheat the oven to 325°F (170°C) Gas 3.

Spread the hazelnuts out on a baking sheet. Toast in the preheated oven for 12 minutes, stirring once. Put the nuts in a clean kitchen towel and rub vigorously until the skins come loose. Shake or blow the loosened skins away, and continue rubbing the nuts until they are mostly free from skins. Roughly chop.

Toss the rice with the hazelnuts, scallions/spring onions, mint, basil, cilantro/coriander, and oil. Scatter with edible petals, if using, to serve.

roasted sweet potato and macadamia nut salad

3 sweet potatoes, about 10 oz./300 g each, peeled

1 tablespoon olive oil

1 teaspoon sea salt flakes

⅓ cup/70 g raw macadamia nuts, roughly chopped

7 oz./200 g baby spinach leaves, washed and patted dry

For the dressing:

1 tablespoon cider vinegar

1 teaspoon wholegrain mustard

2 tablespoons macadamia nut oil or light olive oil

sea salt and freshly ground black pepper

Serves 4

Creamy macadamia nuts add a great crunch to this salad, but can be replaced by any other nuts or even toasted sunflower or pumpkin seeds if you prefer.

Preheat the oven to 375°F (190°C) Gas 5.

Cut the sweet potatoes into 1-inch/2-cm cubes and toss in a bowl with the olive oil and salt flakes. Tip onto a baking sheet and roast in the preheated oven for 10 minutes.

Put the macadamia nuts in the bowl and toss with any residual oil. Add to the sweet potatoes and roast in the hot oven for 10 minutes, giving the sweet potatoes 20 minutes in total.

To make the dressing, mix together the vinegar, mustard, and macadamia nut oil in a small bowl. Season to taste with salt and pepper.

Arrange the spinach leaves on a serving platter and top with the sweet potatoes and macadamia nuts. Drizzle or spoon the dressing over the top and serve immediately.

main dishes

stir-fried tofu with crisp greens and mushrooms

10½ oz./300 g soft tofu, cubed

8 dried Chinese mushrooms

2 garlic cloves

2 oz./55 g sugar snap peas, trimmed

2 oz./55 g snowpeas/mangetout, trimmed

2 bunches of fine asparagus, cut into short lengths

¼ cup/65 ml vegetable oil or peanut oil

1 tablespoon light soy sauce

a pinch of sugar

a pinch of ground white pepper

sea salt

steamed jasmine rice, to serve (optional)

Serves 4

This stir-fry is very fresh and typically Thai in its simplicity. Although soft tofu runs the risk of breaking up, it's preferable to the firm variety as its creamier, more silky texture goes well here with crispy spring vegetables.

Put the tofu cubes on a plate lined with several layers of paper towels and leave for 20–30 minutes, to allow the towels to absorb excess moisture.

Put the mushrooms in a heatproof bowl and cover with boiling water. Set aside for 20 minutes. Drain the mushrooms, remove the stems and halve any larger ones.

Put the garlic in a mortar with a good pinch of sea salt and pound to a paste with a pestle.

Blanch the vegetables in boiling water for 30 seconds, until bright emerald green and softened. Rinse well under cold water until completely cold.

Heat a wok over high heat, then add the oil. Cook the tofu cubes in the hot oil for 5 minutes, turning often, until light golden and puffed. Transfer the tofu to a plate lined with fresh paper towels and pour off all but 2 tablespoons of oil from the wok. Add the vegetables to the wok and stir-fry for 2 minutes. Add the mushrooms and gently stir-fry for 1 minute. Add the garlic paste and stir-fry for 1 minute, then add the soy sauce, pepper, sugar, and 2 tablespoons water to the wok. Return the tofu to the wok and stir-fry gently for 1 minute to coat all the ingredients in the sauce, being careful not to break up the tofu. Remove the wok from the heat and serve the stir-fried tofu with steamed jasmine rice, if liked.

pan-roasted carrots with barley risotto

2 tablespoons light olive oil

12 baby carrots, ends trimmed

3 tablespoons vegan margarine

2 sprigs of fresh thyme

2 garlic cloves, unpeeled and halved

2 cups/500 ml vegetable stock

1 tablespoon light soy sauce

1½ cups/220 g barley

3 heaping tablespoons vegan Parmesan substitute (such as Parma) or nutritional yeast (optional)

sea salt and freshly ground black pepper

Serves 4

Barley is a wonderful ingredient—it's so unprocessed and earthy. It is used here to make a dish much like a risotto, but without all the stirring! The miso adds an intensely savory flavor that's perfect with the sweetness of the carrots.

Heat the oil in a skillet/frying pan until very hot. Add the carrots and cook for 8–10 minutes, turning every 2 minutes, until golden. Add 2 tablespoons of the margarine, thyme, and garlic to the pan with ½ cup/125 ml water and season well with salt and pepper. Cover the skillet with a tight-fitting lid and cook over medium heat for 15–20 minutes, turning often, until the carrots are tender.

Meanwhile, to make the barley risotto, put the stock and soy sauce in a saucepan with 4 cups/1 litre water and bring to a boil. Add the barley and cook for 45–50 minutes, stirring often, until the barley is soft but not breaking up. Stir in the remaining margarine and vegan Parmesan, if using. Serve the carrots on top of the barley.

Variation:

The cooked carrots could be served hot on a bed of couscous or left to cool and tossed in a salad with beets and toasted pine nuts.

vegetable stir-fry
with szechuan peppercorns

1 teaspoon Szechuan peppercorns,*
plus extra to serve

2 tablespoons peanut oil

4 scallions/spring onions, chopped

2 garlic cloves, sliced

1 small red bell pepper, seeded and
finely sliced lengthwise

1 carrot, finely sliced lengthwise
into matchsticks

18 baby corn (candle corn), chopped
into 3 pieces

freshly squeezed juice of ½ a lemon

3–4 tablespoons dark soy sauce,
or wheat-free tamari

1 small head of broccoli, broken
into florets

14 sugar snap peas, trimmed

1 tablespoon toasted sesame oil

noodles or rice to serve (optional)

Serves 4

Szechuan peppercorns are an important spice in Chinese cookery, included in the well-known blend of five spices. They are readily available in Chinese stores. Serve this dish with rice noodles or steamed rice, as preferred.

Discard any shiny black inner seeds from the peppercorns. Toast the popporcorns in a small skillet/frying pan over low heat for 1–2 minutes until aromatic. Using a mortar and pestle, grind to a coarse powder.

Heat the peanut oil in a wok and add the scallions/spring onions and garlic. Stir-fry over medium-high heat for 1 minute. Add the pepper, carrot, baby corn, lemon juice, and 1 tablespoon of the soy sauce and stir-fry for 2–3 minutes.

Add the broccoli, sugar snap peas, ground Szechuan pepper, and the remaining soy sauce. Stir-fry briefly, cover and cook for 4–5 minutes or until the vegetables are tender but still firm. Uncover and add the sesame oil. Stir and serve hot with noodles or rice, if liked.

*Note: If you can't find Szechuan peppercorns, there is really no substitute. However, you can easily obtain a peppery bite with regular peppercorns. Try a mixture of pink, green, and black for a bit of variety, and add some freshly grated ginger to the stir-fry.

spiced eggplant couscous

¼ cup/65 ml vegetable oil

1 large eggplant/aubergine, cubed

1 tablespoon light olive oil

1⅓ cups/280 g couscous

½ teaspoon paprika

½ teaspoon chili powder

1½ cups/375 ml vegetable stock

1 small bunch of cilantro/fresh coriander, leaves and stems, roughly chopped

2 large handfuls of baby spinach

lemon wedges, to serve

Serves 4

For this dish, rich with Moroccan spices, you will need one large eggplant/aubergine, so look for one that is firm, full, and heavy with shiny deep-purple skin. The couscous recipe alone is a treat and can be enjoyed on its own.

Heat the vegetable oil in skillet frying pan over high heat and cook the cubed eggplant/aubergine for 3–4 minutes, turning often so it is an even, golden brown all over. Place on paper towels to drain off the excess oil.

Heat the olive oil in a saucepan over medium heat. Add the couscous, paprika, and chili powder and cook for 2 minutes, stirring constantly. Add the stock and bring to a boil. Remove the pan from the heat, cover with a tight-fitting lid, and let stand for 10 minutes.

Fluff the couscous with a fork, then cover and leave for a further 5 minutes. Place the couscous in a large bowl and add the eggplant/aubergine, cilantro/coriander, and spinach and toss to combine.

Spoon onto serving plates and serve with lemon wedges on the side for squeezing.

Variation:

Replace the eggplant/aubergine with zucchini/courgettes, cut into rounds. Pan-fry them in a little light olive oil until golden on both sides. Add the zucchini/courgettes to the prepared couscous with a handful of roughly chopped fresh mint.

perfumed Persian pulow

¼ teaspoon ground cinnamon

¼ teaspoon ground cardamom (preferably white, made only from the seeds, not the pods)

½ teaspoon sugar

1¾ cups/350 g basmati rice

1 teaspoon fine sea salt

3 tablespoons light olive oil

⅓ cup/50 g raisins, soaked in warm water for 5 minutes

⅓ cup/25 g slivered/flaked almonds, toasted in a dry skillet/frying pan

¼ cup/25 g shelled unsalted pistachio nuts, coarsely chopped

¾ cup/100 g frozen peas, thawed and blanched in boiling water

1 tablespoon finely grated orange peel

a large pinch of saffron threads, soaked in 2 tablespoons hot water and 2 tablespoons orange flower water

Serves 4–6

Iranians are undoubtedly the greatest rice cooks. Their sophisticated cuisine dates back to the ancient Persian Empire, which wooed its conquered lands with delicious food. Use only basmati rice for this dish, or it will disappoint.

Mix the cinnamon, cardamom, and sugar in a small bowl and set aside. Mix the raisins, almonds, pistachios, and peas in a second bowl and set aside.

Put the rice into a strainer/sieve and rinse under cold running water until the water runs clear. Transfer to a large bowl, cover with fresh cold water and soak for 2 hours. Drain well. Put about 5 cups/1.25 litres water into a large saucepan, bring to a boil, add a pinch of salt, then the rice. Return to the boil and cook for 3–4 minutes without stirring. Drain well and rinse briefly in warm water.

Heat the oil in the same saucepan, then reduce the heat as low as possible. Add layers of ingredients in the following order—a layer of rice, a layer of the raisin-nut-and-pea mixture, a pinch of orange peel, then a pinch of the spice-and-sugar mixture. Repeat this layering pattern until all the ingredients have been used, finishing with a layer of rice.

Sprinkle with the saffron and its soaking liquid. Using the end of a wooden spoon, poke a few holes in the rice all the way down to the bottom of the pan. Cover tightly with a lid lined with a kitchen towel, so that no steam escapes. Cook over very low heat for about 20 minutes—or leave it on super-low for even longer. When ready to serve, remove from the heat, lift the lid and towel and fluff up with a fork. Serve hot.

orange vegetable pilau

2 tablespoons light olive oil

1 onion, chopped

2 garlic cloves, chopped

1 tablespoon finely grated fresh ginger

1 large red chile, finely chopped

1 teaspoon ground coriander

1 teaspoon ground cumin

1 teaspoon turmeric

½ cup/50 g slivered/flaked almonds

1½ cups/300 g basmati rice

1 carrot, cut into large chunks

7 oz./200 g pumpkin or butternut squash, peeled, seeded, and cut into wedges

1 small sweet potato, peeled and cut into thick semi-circles

freshly squeezed juice of 1 lime

a handful of cilantro/fresh coriander leaves, chopped

Serves 4

Although this technique of cooking rice is Middle Eastern in origin, it has spread far and wide—similar rice dishes can be found in European, Asian, Latin American, Caribbean, and Indian cuisines, and it is known by many names including pilaf.

Put the oil in a heavy-based saucepan set over high heat. Add the onion, garlic, ginger, and chile and cook for 5 minutes, stirring often. Add the spices and almonds and cook for a further 5 minutes, until the spices become aromatic and look very dark in the pan.

Add the rice and cook for 1 minute, stirring well to coat the rice in the spices. Add the carrot, pumpkin, and sweet potato to the pan. Pour in 2½ cups/600 ml water and stir well, loosening any grains of rice that are stuck to the bottom of the pan. Bring to a boil, then reduce the heat to low, cover with a tight-fitting lid and cook for 25 minutes, stirring occasionally.

When the rice is tender, take the pan off the heat and add the lime juice and coriander. Stir well to combine and serve hot.

creamy vegetable and cashew nut curry

2 tablespoons vegetable oil

¾ cup/125 g large, unsalted cashews

6 shallots, peeled and halved

1 teaspoon black mustard seeds

6–8 curry leaves

2 garlic cloves, chopped

1 tablespoon finely grated fresh ginger

1 teaspoon turmeric

4 large dried red chiles

1 small red bell pepper, thinly sliced

2 ripe tomatoes, quartered

8 very small new potatoes, halved

14-oz./400-ml can coconut milk

steamed or boiled basmati rice,
to serve

Serves 4

The vibrant colors of Kerala, India's southern-most state, are all here on a plate. This deliciously creamy curry is made even richer with the addition of that irresistably moreish and nutritious treat, the cashew nut.

Put the oil in a heavy-based saucepan set over medium heat. Add the cashews and shallots and cook for 5 minutes, stirring often, until the nuts are just starting to brown.

Add the mustard seeds and curry leaves and cook until the seeds start to pop. Add the garlic, ginger, turmeric, chiles, and red bell pepper to the pan and stir-fry for 2 minutes, until aromatic.

Add the tomatoes, potatoes, and coconut milk, partially cover the pan and let simmer gently over low heat for about 20 minutes, or until the potatoes are cooked through. Spoon over basmati rice to serve.

eggplant, tomato, and red lentil curry

3 tablespoons light olive oil

1 large eggplant/aubergine, cut into 8 pieces

1 red onion, chopped

2 garlic cloves, chopped

1 tablespoon finely chopped fresh ginger

8 oz./250 g cherry tomatoes on the vine

6–8 curry leaves

1 teaspoon ground cumin

¼ teaspoon chili powder

1 tablespoon tomato paste/purée

⅔ cup/125 g red split lentils

a handful of cilantro/coriander leaves, roughly chopped

boiled or steamed basmati rice, to serve

Serves 4

So many iconic international meat-free dishes are based on the eggplant/aubergine, such as the spicy Middle Eastern dip baba ghanoush, Sicilian caponata and the French classic ratatouille.

Heat the oil in a skillet/frying pan set over high heat. When the oil is smoking hot add the eggplant/aubergine to the pan and cook for 5 minutes, turning the pieces often so that they cook evenly. At first it will absorb the oil, but as it cooks to a dark and golden color, the oil will start to seep out back into the pan. Remove the eggplant/aubergine from the pan at this point and not before.

Add the remaining oil, onions, garlic, and ginger to the pan and cook for 5 minutes. Add the cherry tomatoes and cook for 1 minute, until they just soften and collapse, then remove them from the pan before they break up too much and set aside with the eggplant/aubergine.

Add the curry leaves and cumin to the pan and cook for a few minutes, as the curry leaves pop and crackle. Add the chili powder, tomato paste/purée, 2 cups/500 ml water, and the lentils and simmer for 15–20 minutes, until the lentils are tender but retain some bite. Stir in the eggplant/aubergine and cherry tomatoes and cook the curry for a couple of minutes just to warm through. Stir in the cilantro/coriander and spoon over basmati rice to serve.

quick potato and vegetable curry

3 tablespoons peanut or safflower/sunflower oil

1 onion, sliced

2 garlic cloves, chopped

1-inch/3-cm piece of fresh ginger, peeled and grated

1 tablespoon hot red curry paste

1 teaspoon ground cinnamon

1 lb./450 g potatoes, cut into cubes

14-oz./400-g can chopped tomatoes

1¼ cups/300 ml vegetable stock

1 tablespoon tomato paste/purée

8 oz./200 g button mushrooms, halved

8 oz./200 g frozen peas

¼ cup/25 g finely ground almonds*

2 tablespoons chopped cilantro/fresh coriander leaves

sea salt and freshly ground black pepper

boiled basmati rice and warmed naan breads, to serve

Serves 4

This cheat's recipe is quick and easy to prepare as it uses a ready-made curry paste. Be sure to read the labeling on the paste that you choose to ensure that it is suitable for vegans. Serve with boiled basmati rice and warmed naan breads.

Heat the oil in a saucepan and fry the onion, garlic, ginger, curry paste, and cinnamon for 5 minutes. Add the potatoes, tomatoes, stock, tomato paste/purée, salt, and pepper. Bring to a boil, cover, and simmer gently for 20 minutes.

Add the mushrooms, peas, ground almonds, and cilantro/coriander to the pan and cook for a further 10 minutes. Taste and adjust the seasoning with salt and pepper, then serve hot spooned over basmati rice.

*Note: If you can't find ground almonds, use blanched whole almonds and grind them with a mortar and pestle or in a small blender.

ratatouille

3 tablespoons olive oil

1 onion, sliced

3 garlic cloves, crushed

a small bunch of fresh flat-leaf parsley, chopped

1 large eggplant/aubergine, chopped

2–3 red and/or yellow bell peppers, seeded and chopped

4 zucchini/courgettes, sliced

¼ teaspoon sea salt

14-oz./400-g can peeled whole plum tomatoes

2 teaspoons red wine vinegar or balsamic vinegar

sea salt and freshly ground black pepper

rice or couscous, to serve (optional)

Serves 6

Ratatouille is such a simple-to-make and versatile vegetable dish. Serve it with nutty wild rice or couscous for a quick and satisfying meal, or add a pinch of chili powder to leftovers and serve them reheated and wrapped in a tortilla, Mexican style.

Heat the oil in a large, heavy-based saucepan set over medium heat. Add the onion, garlic, and parsley and sauté for 10 minutes, stirring regularly.

Add the eggplant/aubergine and cook for 5 minutes. Add the bell peppers and zucchini/courgettes and stir in the salt. Cook for a few minutes, then add the tomatoes.

Cover and cook for 5 minutes until the tomatoes start to break down, then uncover and cook for 10–15 minutes until the vegetables are tender, adding a little water if necessary. Season to taste with vinegar and salt and pepper. Serve warm with rice or couscous, if liked.

paella of summer vine vegetables with almonds

a large pinch of saffron threads

⅓ cup/80 ml olive oil

7 oz./200 g red or yellow cherry tomatoes

4 oz./115 g green beans

4 baby zucchini/courgettes, halved

3 oz./80 g freshly shelled peas

2 garlic cloves, chopped

2 rosemary sprigs

1½ cups/300 g Arborio risotto rice

3⅓ cups/800 ml vegetable stock

¼ cup/30 g slivered/flaked almonds, lightly toasted

Serves 4

This is a new take on the classic Spanish rice dish. It's colorful, delicious, and bursting with fresh, young vegetables grown on the vine and enhanced with a subtle hint of saffron. Perfect for summer entertaining.

Put the saffron in a bowl with ⅓ cup/65 ml hot water and set aside to infuse. Heat half of the oil in a heavy-based skillet/frying pan set over high heat and add the tomatoes. Cook for 2 minutes, shaking the pan so that the tomatoes soften and start to split. Use a slotted spoon to remove the tomatoes from the pan and set aside. Add the beans, zucchini/courgettes, and peas and stir-fry over high heat for 2–3 minutes. Set aside with the tomatoes until needed.

Add the remaining oil to the pan with the garlic and rosemary and cook gently for 1 minute to infuse the oil. Add the rice to the pan and cook, stirring constantly, for 2 minutes, until the rice is glossy and opaque. Add the stock and saffron-infused water to the pan. Stir just once or twice, then increase the heat and let the liquid reach a boil. When the stock is rapidly boiling and little holes have formed in the rice, reduce the heat to medium and let simmer gently for about 20 minutes, until almost all the liquid has been absorbed.

Scatter the cooked tomatoes, beans, zucchini/courgettes, and peas over the rice, cover lightly with some foil and cook over low heat for 5 minutes so that the vegetables are just heated through. Sprinkle the toasted almonds on top to serve.

barley risotto with greens, radicchio, and leeks

1¼ cups/220 g pearl barley

3 tablespoons light olive oil

1 lb./450 g spring greens (collards), roughly chopped

4 large radicchio leaves, torn

finely grated peel and freshly squeezed juice of 1 lemon

5 cups/1.25 litres vegetable stock

1 leek, thinly sliced

2 garlic cloves, chopped

2 teaspoons fresh thyme leaves

1 tablespoon fresh rosemary needles

sea salt and freshly ground black pepper

a handful of fresh flat-leaf parsley, roughly chopped

Serves 4

You will see spring greens and radicchio displayed side by side at farmers' markets. When used raw in salads radicchio can be a little too bitter, but when cooked in this risotto its flavour is softened and the barley adds a nice nutty note.

Put the barley in a large, heatproof bowl and add sufficient boiling water to cover. Let sit for 10 minutes, just to soften the barley a little, then drain well and set aside.

Put the 2 tablespoons of the oil in a skillet/frying pan set over medium heat. Add the greens and radicchio and cook for 10 minutes, stirring often, until the leaves soften. Add the lemon zest and juice, stir well, and set aside. Put the stock in a large saucepan set over low heat and gently warm through while you start the risotto.

Put the remaining tablespoonful of the oil in a saucepan set over medium heat. Add the leek and garlic and cook for 4–5 minutes until the leeks are soft and silky. Add the barley and herbs and stir for 1 minute. Add a ladleful of the warmed stock and cook, stirring constantly, until almost all the stock has been absorbed. Repeat the process until all the stock has been incorporated and the barley is almost cooked through—the risotto will be quite wet. Add the greens and radicchio to the pan and stir well to combine. Season to taste with salt and pepper, sprinkle with parsley and serve hot.

Calabrian-style potatoes and bell peppers

⅔ cup/150 ml olive oil

1 red bell pepper, halved, seeded, and thickly sliced

1 yellow bell pepper, halved, seeded, and thickly sliced

1¼ lbs./550 g potatoes, thinly sliced

sea salt and freshly ground black pepper

a small bunch of fresh flat-leaf parsley, finely chopped

Serves 4

This is a fine example of the "less is more" approach to cooking vegetables—simple, good-quality ingredients cooked to perfection. Use waxy potatoes that will hold their shape during cooking and the biggest bell peppers you can find.

Heat the oil in a large, lidded skillet/frying pan. Add the red and yellow bell peppers and cook for 10 minutes, stirring occasionally, until starting to turn golden brown. Add the potatoes to the pan, season with salt and pepper, cover with the lid, and cook for 5 minutes.

Remove the lid and continue cooking for a further 15 minutes, turning every few minutes as the potatoes begin to brown, taking care not to break them. If the potatoes start to stick, this will just add to the flavor of the dish, but don't let them burn.

When the potatoes are tender, transfer to a serving dish and top with the parsley, if using. Let cool for 5 minutes before serving.

imam bayildi

⅔ cup/150 ml extra virgin olive oil

3 medium eggplants/aubergines, rinsed and halved lengthwise

sea salt and freshly ground black pepper

For the stuffing:

2 onions, finely chopped

4 garlic cloves, finely chopped

1 teaspoon ground cumin

1 lb./450 g ripe tomatoes, chopped

1 tablespoon dried oregano

½ teaspoon sugar

3 tablespoons chopped fresh flat-leaf parsley

1 tablespoon tomato paste/purée, diluted with ⅔ cup/150 ml hot water

Serves 6

This Turkish dish derives it's name from an old fable about the priest (Imam) who fainted either from over-indulging in this rich dish or in shock because of the extravagant amount of olive oil used! It tastes even better served at room temperature.

Preheat the oven to 375°F (190°C) Gas 5.

Heat half the olive oil in a large skillet/frying pan, add 3 pieces of the eggplant/aubergine and shallow-fry for about 10–15 minutes, turning them over, until light golden on both sides. Remove and rest on paper towels. Repeat with the remaining 3 pieces. Arrange them side by side in a shallow ovenproof dish and season well with salt and pepper.

To make the stuffing, heat the remaining olive oil in a saucepan, add the onions and sauté gently until they start to color. Add the garlic and cumin, fry for 2–3 minutes, then add the tomatoes, oregano, and sugar. Pour in ⅔ cup/165 ml water and season with salt and pepper. Cover and cook for 15 minutes, stirring occasionally.

Stir in the parsley, then divide the stuffing into 6 equal portions. Pile each portion along the length of each eggplant/aubergine half. Pour the diluted tomato paste/purée into the dish and cook in the preheated oven for about 45 minutes, basting the eggplants/aubergines once during cooking. Serve hot or, better still, at room temperature.

okra with tomato and dried limes

2 lbs./800 g fresh okra

⅔ cup/150 ml extra virgin olive oil

1 large onion, sliced

1 teaspoon ground coriander

½ teaspoon ground allspice

14-oz./400-g can chopped tomatoes

2 dried limes

½ teaspoon sugar

2 tablespoons finely chopped
cilantro/fresh coriander

sea salt and freshly ground
black pepper

Serves 6

With its lush intriguing taste, okra is the beloved vegetable of the Eastern Mediterranean. The dried limes, which can be obtained from Arab or Indian stores, add an altogether new dimension to its sweet taste.

To prepare the okra, pare the conical tops with a sharp knife (similar to peeling potatoes.) Put in a bowl, cover with cold water briefly, then drain, handling with care.

Heat the oil in a large saucepan, add the onion and sauté until light golden. Add the ground coriander and allspice, then when aromatic, add the tomatoes, dried limes, and sugar and season well with salt and pepper. Cook for 10 minutes, pressing the limes with a spatula to extract their sour juices.

Add the okra and spread evenly in the pan. Add enough hot water until they are almost immersed in the sauce.

Cook gently for about 30 minutes, shaking the pan occasionally but don't stir as okra is fragile. Sprinkle the cilantro/coriander over the top and simmer for 5–10 minutes more. Serve warm or at room temperature.

tourlou

2 small eggplants/aubergines

1¾ lbs./800 g plum tomatoes

1 fennel bulb

2 large onions

4 garlic cloves, sliced

1 lb./450 g small zucchini/courgettes, cut into thick rounds

2 waxy potatoes, cut into wedges

⅓ cup/75 ml extra virgin olive oil

1 tablespoon coarse sea salt

freshly ground black pepper

several sprigs of thyme

a few sage leaves

a small handful of fresh flat-leaf parsley, chopped

grilled pitta breads, to serve

Serves 4

This popular Cypriot recipe is basically any mixed roasted vegetables, but this is a particularly good combination. You can vary the vegetables as you like, but tomatoes are important—without them, the mixture can be a little dry.

Preheat the oven to 425°F (220°C) Gas 7.

Quarter the eggplants/aubergines lengthwise, then cut into ½ inch/1.5 cm pieces. To degorge, put the pieces in a large glass bowl with a few spoonfuls of water and microwave on HIGH for 4 minutes. Drain off the excess liquid and set aside.

To prepare the remaining vegetables, cut the tomatoes in 4, trim the stems from the fennel, then halve the bulb and cut into slices. Cut each onion into 6 wedges. Put all the vegetables in a large roasting pan/tin. Add the oil, salt, pepper, and herbs and mix well with your hands. Spread in an even layer.

Roast in the preheated oven for 20 minutes, then mix well. Continue roasting for a further 30–35 minutes, until the vegetables are tender. Serve hot or at room temperature with grilled pitta bread.

Spanish stuffed peppers

6 oz./185 g canned peeled piquillo peppers or pimientos

¼ cup/60 ml olive oil

3–4 garlic cloves, chopped

2 cups/550 g canned white beans, such as cannellini or butter beans, part-drained (reserve the liquid)

2 tablespoons good sherry vinegar, plus a little extra to serve

a handful of fresh thyme leaves, finely chopped

sea salt and freshly ground black pepper

a few handfuls of mixed baby salad leaves, to serve

Serves 4

Piquillo peppers are vividly red, mildly spicy-hot, often sold roasted and peeled in cans or jars. Buy piquillo peppers from Hispanic stores and good delis. Serve with a good chilled fino or amontillado sherry, baby salad greens, and crusty bread.

Drain the piquillo peppers, reserving the liquid. Pat dry with paper towels.

Heat the oil, garlic, and part-drained white beans in a non-stick skillet/frying pan and mash with a fork to a thick, coarse purée. Add 1 tablespoon of the sherry vinegar and 1 tablespoon of bean liquid, stir, then season well with salt and pepper. Let cool slightly, then stuff each piquillo with the mixture and sprinkle with the thyme.

Cut each piquillo into thick slices or leave whole. Arrange on serving plates, adding some salad leaves to each. Trickle over a tablespoonful of the preserving liquid and a few more drops of vinegar to serve. Serve warm.

Variation:

Instead of canned piquillos or pimientos, you could use 4 sweet long red bell peppers (romano), halved lengthwise and seeded. Grill them until blistered. Rub off the skins, stuff with the bean mixture, roll up, then serve as in the main recipe.

grilled chile-marinated zucchini

6 zucchini/courgettes, ends trimmed
extra virgin olive oil, for brushing

For the chile marinade:
½ cup/125 ml olive oil
3 tablespoons balsamic vinegar
3 tablespoons sherry vinegar
1 tablespoon coarse sea salt
1 fresh red chile, seeded and
finely chopped
1 tablespoon dried oregano
2 garlic cloves, finely chopped
freshly ground black pepper

a ridged stovetop grill pan
a pastry brush

Serves 4–6

This recipe is good simply served with olives and crusty bread. Any leftovers can be used as a sandwich filling with hummus or tossed with pasta. Other vegetables can be prepared in the same way: bell peppers are good, as are mushrooms.

To make the marinade, put the olive oil in a large, shallow non-metal dish. Add both the vinegars, salt, chile, oregano, garlic, and pepper and mix well.

Slice the zucchini/courgettes into long strips, about ½ inch/6–7 mm thick, using a mandolin if you have one. Pour the olive oil into a small bowl.

Heat the grill pan until hot. Working in batches, brush the zucchini/courgette slices with olive oil on one side and arrange in the pan at a slight angle, oiled-side down, until the pan is full. Cook until charred, 2–3 minutes. Brush the top side with oil, turn them over and cook until the other side is also charred, 2–3 minutes more.

Using tongs, transfer the zucchini/courgette slices to the marinade. Continue cooking until all the zucchini/courgettes have been grilled. They should have char marks but shouldn't be completely cooked through.

Cover and set aside at room temperature for 3–4 hours or refrigerate overnight (return to room temperature before serving). Turn them in the marinade occasionally, so they soak up as much as possible.

tagine of root vegetables with prunes

2 tablespoons vegan margarine

1 tablespoon olive oil

2 onions, cut into wedges

9 oz./250 g yams, peeled and chopped

9 oz./250 g sweet potatoes, peeled and cut into large chunks

9 oz./250 g baby carrots, scrubbed or peeled if necessary

9 oz./250 g parsnips, peeled and cut into large chunks

1 tablespoon maple syrup or agave nectar

2 tablespoons grated fresh ginger

1 cinnamon stick, broken in half

⅓ cup/100 g pitted prunes

2 cups/500 ml vegetable stock

sea salt and freshly ground black pepper

crusty bread, rice, or couscous, to serve

a tagine or flameproof lidded casserole dish

Serves 6

Serve this fragrant and warming Moroccan-style vegetable stew with plenty of crusty bread to soak up the tasty juices, or with nutty brown rice or, best of all with the more traditional accompaniment of couscous.

Preheat the oven to 350°F (180°C) Gas 4.

Heat the margarine and oil in a tagine or flameproof lidded casserole dish. Add the onions and cook for 5 minutes until softened.

Add the yams, sweet potatoes, carrots, and parsnips and cook, stirring occasionally, for 5 minutes. Add the maple syrup, ginger, cinnamon stick, and prunes and season to taste with salt and pepper. Pour in the stock.

Cover and bake in the preheated oven for 45 minutes, uncovering for the final 15 minutes of cooking. Serve warm with bread, rice, or couscous, as preferred.

grilled vegetable and almond couscous with herb dressing

1½ cups/375 ml vegetable stock

1 cup/175 g couscous

2 garlic cloves, crushed

finely grated peel of 2 lemons

4 tablespoons olive oil

2 red bell peppers, seeded and thickly sliced

3 zucchini/courgettes, sliced lengthwise and then diagonally across

1 eggplant/aubergine, cut into slices ½ inch/1 cm thick

1 red onion, cut into wedges

1 cup/150 g almonds, toasted

sea salt and freshly ground black pepper

For the herb dressing:

3 tablespoons cider vinegar

leaves from a small bunch of fresh flat-leaf parsley, finely chopped

leaves from a small bunch of fresh mint, finely chopped

2 tablespoons chopped fresh oregano

2 tablespoons finely chopped chives

6 tablespoons olive oil

sea salt and freshly ground black pepper

a ridged stovetop grill pan

Serves 6

Couscous is an ideal solution for those preparing a meal in a hurry, as it's incredibly fast and simple. Here the couscous is mixed with grilled vegetables and served with a tangy herb dressing and a scattering of crunchy almonds.

To make the herb dressing, whisk together the vinegar and oil in a small bowl and add all the herbs. Mix well to combine and season to taste with salt and pepper. Set aside until needed.

Bring the stock to a boil in a large saucepan, then stir in the couscous. Remove from the heat, cover and leave to absorb the stock for 10 minutes. Season to taste with salt and pepper and then fluff up well with a fork.

Meanwhile, combine the garlic and lemon peel with 2 tablespoons of the oil in a small bowl and season to taste with salt and pepper.

Heat the grill pan to hot. Put the bell peppers, zucchini/courgettes, eggplant/aubergine, and onion in a bowl with the remaining 2 tablespoons of oil and toss to coat. Cook the vegetables in the grill pan for about 3 minutes on each side, until tender. Cut the cooked eggplant/aubergine slices into quarters and place in a large bowl with the other vegetables. Add the couscous and almonds and toss to combine.

Spoon the mixture onto a warmed serving platter and spoon over the herb dressing to serve.

root vegetable ragu
with spiced couscous

3 tablespoons olive oil

1 tablespoon margarine

1 red onion, chopped

1 celery rib/stick, roughly chopped

6 garlic cloves, lightly smashed

2 cups/500 ml passata (Italian sieved tomatoes)

2 cups/500 ml vegetable stock

2 tablespoons fresh oregano leaves

1 parsnip, peeled and chopped

2 carrots, peeled and chopped

6 small, waxy new potatoes

For the spiced couscous:

1½ cups/375 ml vegetable stock

2 tablespoons vegan margarine

2 cups/280 g couscous

1 teaspoon ground cumin

1 teaspoon ground coriander

1 teaspoon *pimentón dulce* (Spanish smoked sweet paprika)

¼ teaspoon cayenne pepper

Serves 4

This is a hearty dish packed with nutritious root veggies. This method for making couscous is not the traditional Moroccan way, but it does produce a full-flavored version that makes the perfect accompaniment to the rich ragu.

Put the oil and margarine in a large saucepan set over high heat. When the margarine sizzles, add the onion, celery, and garlic. Reduce the heat to medium, partially cover the pan, and cook for 10 minutes, stirring often, until the vegetables are soft and lightly browned. Add the passata, stock, and oregano and bring to a boil. Reduce the heat to a medium simmer and cook, uncovered, for about 20 minutes. Add the parsnip, carrots, and potatoes to the pan and cook for a further 15–20 minutes until tender.

To make the spiced couscous, put the stock and margarine in a small saucepan set over high heat. Bring to a boil, then reduce the heat to low and keep the stock warm. Put the couscous and spices in a medium, heavy based saucepan and cook over medium/high heat until the spices are aromatic and just start to turn a dusky brown. Turn off the heat. Pour the warm stock into the pan. Stir, cover with a tight-fitting lid, and let sit for 10 minutes. Fluff up the couscous with a fork, cover again, and let sit for a further 5 minutes. Tip the couscous out into a bowl and fluff up to separate as many grains as possible. Spoon onto serving plates, top with the root vegetable ragu and serve.

seven-vegetable tagine with quinoa

2 teaspoons ground cumin

2 teaspoons ground coriander

a pinch of saffron threads

1 cinnamon stick or ½ teaspoon ground cinnamon

2 garlic cloves, crushed

1 tablespoon grated fresh ginger

1 onion, thinly sliced

grated peel and freshly squeezed juice of 1 lemon

2 carrots, diced

4 oz./115 g small turnips, halved

2½ cups/600 ml boiling water

1 lb./450 g butternut squash, peeled, seeded, and chopped

1 cup/100 g dried apricots

1 eggplant/aubergine, cut into dice

1 teaspoon olive oil

2 zucchini/courgettes, chopped

2 tomatoes, quartered

sea salt and freshly ground black pepper

To serve:

1⅓ cups/200 g quinoa

1¾ cups/400 ml boiling water

a pinch of sea salt

a large tagine or flameproof lidded casserole dish

Serves 4

Quinoa (pronounced keen-wa) is a South American supergrain that has a high protein content, making it a good choice for a vegan diet. The grains are cooked in the same way as rice but guadruple in size, becoming almost transparent.

Preheat the oven to 400°F (200°C) Gas 6.

Put the spices in the tagine or casserole dish with the garlic, ginger, onion, and lemon zest and juice. Add the carrots, turnips, and boiling water, stir well and bring to a simmer. Cover and cook for 5 minutes.

Once the tagine is underway, put the quinoa in a saucepan with the boiling water and salt. Bring to a boil, stir once, then cover, reduce the heat, and cook gently for 15 minutes until the quinoa is tender and has absorbed all the liquid.

Stir the butternut squash and apricots into the tagine, re-cover and cook for a further 10 minutes. Meanwhile, toss the eggplant/aubergine with the olive oil, season with salt and pepper, spread out on a baking sheet and roast in the preheated oven for 15 minutes until softened and golden brown.

Add the zucchini/courgettes and tomatoes to the tagine, cover again and cook for a further 5 minutes. Mix the roasted eggplants/aubergines into the tagine and serve spooned over the quinoa.

tagliatelle with pan-fried pumpkin and red pepper oil

1 tablespoon light olive oil

1 lb./450 g pumpkin or butternut squash, peeled, seeded, and chopped

14 oz./400 g vegan-friendly tagliatelle or spaghetti (i.e. not egg pasta)

finely grated peel and juice of 1 lemon

a large handful of arugula/rocket

a large handful of chopped fresh flat-leaf parsley

sea salt and freshly ground black pepper

For the red pepper oil:

1 small red bell pepper, sliced

6 large red chiles, sliced

1 small red onion, sliced

4 garlic cloves, peeled but left whole

1 teaspoon cumin seeds

¼ cup/65 ml olive oil

Serves 4

Not all pasta is suitable for vegans so check that what you are using is egg-free and labelled vegan-friendly. The trick to this recipe is to take it slowly—let the bell pepper and chile release their flavor into the oil by roasting in a low oven for a full hour.

Preheat the oven to 350°F (180°C) Gas 4.

Put the red bell pepper, chiles, onion, garlic, cumin seeds, and 2 tablespoons of the olive oil in a roasting pan. Cook in the preheated oven for 1 hour, turning often. Transfer the contents of the pan to a food processor while still hot. Add the remaining oil and whizz until smooth. Let cool, then pour the mixture into a clean and dry screwtop jar.

Heat the light olive oil in a skillet/frying pan set over high and add the pumpkin. Cook for 10 minutes, turning often, until each piece is golden brown all over. Meanwhile, cook the pasta according to the package instructions and drain well. Put it in a large bowl and add 2–3 tablespoons of the red pepper oil. Add the cooked pumpkin, lemon peel and juice, arugula/rocket, and parsley and toss to combine. Season well with salt and pepper and serve immediately.

Note: The remaining red pepper oil will keep for 1 week when stored in an airtight jar in the refrigerator. It can be used as a dip for baked potato wedges or can be used to enrich tomato-based sauces and soups.

smoky hotpot of great northern beans

½ cup/100 g dried great northern
or butter or lima beans

2 tablespoons olive oil

1 large onion, chopped

2 garlic cloves, chopped

2 teaspoons *pimentón dulce* (Spanish
smoked sweet paprika)

1 celery rib/stick, chopped

1 carrot, chopped

2 medium waxy potatoes, cut into dice

1 red bell pepper, chopped

2 cups/500 ml vegetable stock

sea salt and freshly ground
black pepper

crusty bread, to serve

Serves 4

This is a hearty hotpot rich with smoky paprika. Great northern beans are large and white, resembling butter beans in shape but with a distinctive flavor. If you can't find them, large butter beans or lima beans will do just as well.

Soak the dried beans in cold water for at least 6 hours or ideally overnight. Drain and put in a large saucepan with sufficient just-boiled water to cover. Cook for 30 minutes until softened. Drain and set aside until needed.

Put the oil in a saucepan set over medium heat. Add the onion and cook for 4–5 minutes until softened. Add the garlic and pimentón to the pan and stir-fry for 2 minutes. Add the celery, carrot, potatoes, and red bell pepper and cook for 2 minutes, stirring constantly to coat the vegetables in the oil. Add the stock and beans and bring to a boil. Reduce the heat and partially cover the pan with a lid. Let simmer for 40 minutes, stirring often, until all the vegetables are cooked. Season to taste and serve with crusty bread for dipping in the sauce.

roasted vegetables with chickpeas

12 small mushrooms

2 ripe tomatoes, halved

1 red bell pepper, cut into strips

1 yellow bell pepper, cut into strips

1 red onion, cut into wedges

1 small fennel bulb, sliced into
thin wedges

1 garlic bulb, broken into individual
cloves but left unpeeled

2 teaspoons sea salt

2 tablespoons olive oil

14-oz./400-g can chickpeas, drained
and rinsed

2 sprigs of fresh thyme or rosemary

Spiced Couscous (see page 167),
to serve (optional)

Serves 4

**A few chickpeas are all that is needed to turn an unassuming
pan of roasted vegetables into a filing and delicious meal.
Serve with plenty of Spiced Couscous (see page 167) to soak
up the tasty pan juices.**

Preheat the oven to 350°F (180°C) Gas 4.

Put the mushrooms, tomatoes, red and yellow bell peppers, onion, fennel,
and garlic in a large roasting pan. Sprinkle the salt over the vegetables and
drizzle with the oil. Roast in the preheated oven for 1 hour.

Remove the pan from the oven and turn the vegetables. Add the chickpeas
and thyme or rosemary sprigs. Return the pan to the oven and roast for
a further 30 minutes, until the edges of the vegetables are just starting to
blacken and char.

To serve, spoon the spiced couscous (if using) onto serving plates and top
with the warm roasted vegetables with chickpeas.

spiced cauliflower curry with red bell pepper and peas

½ a head of cauliflower, cut into large florets

2 teaspoons ground cumin

1 teaspoon turmeric

3 tablespoons light olive oil

2 teaspoons black mustard seeds

6–8 curry leaves

1 onion, sliced

1 small red bell pepper, thinly sliced

1 tablespoon finely grated fresh ginger

2 garlic cloves, chopped

1 large green chile, sliced

½ cup/125 ml vegetable stock

2 ripe tomatoes, chopped

1 cup/125 g fresh or frozen peas

steamed or boiled basmati rice, to serve (optional)

Serves 4

The vegan recipes you find in Indian cuisine are some of the most delicious in the world. Many of the recipes embrace the philosophy of cooking fresh produce at its best and keeping it simple. This is a spicy treat that's perfect if you like things hot.

Put the cauliflower florets in a large bowl with the cumin and turmeric and toss until evenly coated in the spices.

Put the oil in a skillet/frying pan set over medium/high heat. Add the cauliflower, mustard seeds, and curry leaves and cook for 8–10 minutes, turning the pieces often so that they soften and color with the spices. Add the onion and red bell pepper and cook for 5 minutes. Add the ginger, garlic, and chile and stir-fry for 1 minute, then add the stock, tomatoes, and peas. Reduce the heat and let simmer gently for 10 minutes until the vegetables are tender and cooked through.

Spoon over basmati rice to serve, if liked.

grilled mixed vegetable platter

1 eggplant/aubergine, sliced
4 field mushrooms
1 bunch of thin asparagus spears
1 celery rib/stick, cut into short lengths
1 red bell pepper, cut into strips
brown rice, to serve (optional)

For the marinade:
½ cup/125 ml light soy sauce
¼ cup/65 ml balsamic vinegar
1 tablespoon olive oil
2 teaspoons sugar

Serves 4

You can use pretty much any combination of vegetables that you like here, but it's important to cook them separately, as it's best not to crowd the grill. The marinade also makes a good dressing for any Chinese-style noodle salad.

Put all of the ingredients for the marinade in a small bowl and whisk to combine. Arrange the vegetables in a large, shallow non-metal dish and pour over the marinade. Use your hands to toss the vegetables around until evenly coated in the marinade. Cover with plastic wrap/clingfilm and let sit for 1 hour, turning occasionally.

Preheat a charcoal grill or conventional broiler/grill. Use tongs to transfer the vegetables to a plate and reserve the marinade. Cook the eggplant/aubergine, and mushrooms first, for 2–3 minutes on each side, until dark brown, basting once or twice with a little of the reserved marinade. Transfer to a warmed serving plate. Next cook the asparagus, celery, and red bell pepper for 3–4 minutes on each side, basting with a little of the marinade as necessary. Transfer the vegetables to the serving plate to join the eggplant/aubergine and mushrooms.

Serve the grilled vegetables with brown rice, if liked. Any remaining marinade can be used as a spooning sauce.

baby leeks with sage and chile bread crumbs

6 tablespoons/75 g vegan margarine

2 tablespoons chopped fresh sage

1 lb./450 g short and thin young leeks, washed and trimmed

2 tablespoons extra virgin olive oil

1 cup/50 g fresh ciabatta bread crumbs

1 mild long red chile, seeded and finely chopped

1 smaller red chile, seeded and sliced into rings

Serves 4

Sage makes a great partnership with leeks and the Italian-style chile bread crumb topping makes a delicious combination. For an even more pronounced Italian accent, the crispy crumbs are made from ciabatta bread.

Put the margarine and sage in a bowl and mash well.

Steam or boil the leeks for about 5 minutes, or until tender. Toss in half the sage margarine and keep hot.

Heat a skillet/frying pan, add the oil and bread crumbs and fry for about 45 seconds. Add the remaining sage margarine and all the finely chopped chiles. Fry until golden.

Put the leeks on a serving plate, and top with the chile bread crumbs and the smaller sliced chile.

Variation:

If you are lucky enough to be able to source sea kale or salsify, both these are also good served this way.

oven-roasted vegetables, with rosemary, bay leaves, and garlic

1 lb./450 g potatoes, cut into chunks

1 lb./450 g butternut squash, cut into wedges and seeded

6 small red onions, quartered

4 tablespoons extra virgin olive oil

8 garlic cloves, unpeeled

2 red romano (long) bell peppers, seeded and cut into chunks

1 sprig of rosemary

4 sprigs of bay leaves

sea salt

Serves 4

Roasted vegetables are made extra special with the addition of fresh herbs. Rosemary is good, but don't use too much of it as it can be a little overwhelming. Bay leaves are mild when young, so don't use as many if you have mature leaves.

Preheat the oven to 400°F (200°C) Gas 6.

Bring a large saucepan of water to a boil, add a pinch of salt and the potatoes and cook for 5 minutes. Drain well, then transfer to a large roasting pan. Add the butternut squash, onions, and 2 tablespoons of the oil. Toss to coat, then roast in the preheated oven for 10 minutes.

Add 1 extra tablespoon of oil to the roasting pan, followed by the garlic and bell peppers, 2 sprigs of rosemary, and 2 sprigs of bay leaves. Roast for 15 minutes, then add the rest of the herbs and continue roasting for 10–15 minutes. Turn the vegetables occasionally until they are all tender and the edges slightly charred. Drizzle the remaining oil over the top, then serve.

Variation:

Sprinkle with 3 tablespoons of pine nuts and some crumbled vegan cheese over the vegetables 5 minutes before the end of the cooking time, so the nuts roast a little and the cheese softens.

baked stuffed mushrooms

5 very large portabello mushrooms or
10 large cremini/chestnut mushrooms

2–4 teaspoons extra virgin olive oil

1 rib/stick celery, finely chopped

1–2 large garlic cloves, crushed

1 fresh green chile, seeded and
finely chopped

½ cup/50 g fresh whole-wheat
bread crumbs

1 tomato, seeded and chopped

2 tablespoons freshly snipped chives
plus extra to garnish

sea salt and freshly ground
black pepper

mixed salad leaves, to serve

Serves 4

**Mushrooms are nature's cups just waiting to be filled. This
simple recipe uses garlic, chiles, and chives to give plenty
of taste. You can use either very large portobello mushrooms
or smaller chestnut mushrooms, as preferred.**

Preheat the oven to 350°F (180°C) Gas 4.

Select 4 portobello mushrooms or 8 cremini mushrooms for stuffing.
Remove the stalks from the mushrooms. Put the caps stem-side up in an
ovenproof dish. Finely chop the remaining mushrooms and all the stalks.
Heat a non-stick skillet/frying pan and add 2 teaspoons of the oil. Add the
chopped mushrooms, celery, garlic, and chile and sauté, stirring frequently,
until soft. Let cool slightly, then transfer to a bowl.

Add the bread crumbs, tomato, and chives to the bowl, then season
to taste with salt and pepper. Mix well, adding a little oil to moisten, if
necessary. Fill the mushrooms with the bread crumb mixture. Pour about
4 tablespoons of water into the dish, then cook in the preheated oven for
12–15 minutes, until the mushrooms are soft and the topping is crisp.
Remove from the oven and serve immediately, sprinkled with some chives
and accompanied by mixed salad leaves.

Variation:

For a quick and easy meal, prepare the mushrooms for stuffing as above.
Put the remaining mushrooms with 2 garlic cloves, 2 oz./50 g whole-wheat
bread, 6 scallions/spring onions, 2 oz./50 g dried apricots, 2 tablespoons
pecans, and 2 tablespoons of cilantro/fresh coriander leaves in a food
processor. Season to taste with salt and pepper. Process, adding a little
lemon juice if necessary, to give a moist stuffing. Fill the mushrooms with
this mixture and cook as directed above.

grilled portobello mushrooms
with lemon and olive oil

4 very large portobello mushrooms

For the marinade:

2 tablespoons extra virgin olive oil

1 tablespoon soy sauce

finely grated peel and freshly squeezed juice of 1 lemon

2 garlic cloves, crushed

1 sprig of rosemary

freshly ground black pepper

To serve:

sourdough bread

vegan-friendly horseradish sauce (optional)

*a ridged stovetop grill pan
or charcoal grill*

Serves 4

The earthy, satisfying taste of portobello mushrooms needs very little to improve it. Simple cooking and a complement of good-quality ingredients will reveal their absolute best.

To make the marinade, put the olive oil, soy sauce, lemon peel and juice, garlic, rosemary, and pepper in a bowl and mix well to combine. Arrange the mushrooms in a shallow, non-metal dish. Pour the marinating liquid over them so that they are well covered. Cover with plastic wrap/clingfilm. Set aside to infuse for 30 minutes.

Heat the grill pan until hot, add the mushrooms and cook for 5 minutes on each side or until softened. Alternatively cook on a charcoal grill.

Serve the mushrooms on top of crusty sourdough bread with a smear of horseradish, if using, then pour any remaining marinade juices over the top.

tofu in a hot, sweet, and spicy infusion

8 oz./250 g firm tofu

2 tablespoons hoisin sauce*

3 tablespoons soy sauce

1 red chile, finely chopped

1-inch/2-cm piece of fresh ginger, peeled and grated

1 teaspoon toasted sesame oil

1 tablespoon rice vinegar

a handful of cilantro/fresh coriander, coarsely chopped, to serve

a ridged stovetop grill pan or charcoal grill

Serves 4

Tofu receives some bad press and can be dull and tasteless when served *au naturel*. However, it does act as a sponge for marinades—they percolate all the way through, giving the tofu a fantastic taste. For vegans, it's a good source of protein.

Cut through the cake of tofu horizontally to make 2 thin slices. Cut each slice into 4 pieces.

Put the hoisin, soy sauce, chile, ginger, sesame oil, and rice vinegar in a small bowl and mix well. Pour onto a large plate, then put the tofu on top. Spoon some of the mixture over the top so that the tofu is completely covered. Leave for as long as possible to soak up the marinade, at least 2 hours or overnight.

When ready to cook, put the tofu in a smoking-hot stovetop grill pan, reserving some of the marinade. Cook each side for 4–5 minutes until lightly browned. Alternatively, cook on a hot charcoal grill. Serve immediately with the reserved marinade, topped with cilantro/coriander.

*Note: Although "hoisin" literally translates from the Chinese as "fish", the sauce (also known as Chinese Barbecue Sauce) is actually made from a combination of fermented soy, garlic, vinegar, chiles, and sugar. It has a very strong salty and slightly sweet flavor and is a great way to add authentic Asian character to any vegetable stir-fry or noodle dish.

summer squash infused with mint and balsamic vinegar

1 lb./450 g yellow and green patty pans*, halved

⅓ cup/80 ml extra virgin olive oil

2 tablespoons balsamic vinegar

¾ cup/40 g pine nuts, lightly toasted in a dry skillet/frying pan

a handful of fresh mint leaves, roughly chopped

3 zucchini/courgettes, cut lengthwise into thin slices

sea salt and freshly ground black pepper

crusty bread, to serve

a ridged stovetop grill pan or charcoal grill

Serves 4

This dish looks and tastes sunny and fresh and is perfect for cooking on an outdoor charcoal grill in summer. You can prepare it head of time, then leave it to soak up the oil, mint, and balsamic vinegar. Delicious served with crusty bread.

Heat a stovetop grill pan until smoking hot. Cook the patty pans on each side for about 5 minutes or until tender, turning over when starting to char. Alternatively, cook on a hot charcoal grill.

When cooked, transfer to a serving dish. Pour over the oil and vinegar and sprinkle with pine nuts and mint and season well with salt and pepper.

Cook the sliced zucchini/courgettes in the pan or on the grill, for just 1–2 minutes on each side. Add to the patty pans, turn to coat, cover and let marinate for about 2 hours in the refrigerator, then return to room temperature to serve.

*Note: Patty pans are members of the squash family and are either yellow or green. They look a little alien, rather like mini flying saucers, but taste wonderful. They are available from large supermarkets all summer.

butternut squash with pistou sauce

2 butternut squash, weighing
about 2 lbs./800 g each

For the pistou sauce:
6 tablespoons extra virgin olive oil
4 garlic cloves
a large handful of fresh basil leaves
sea salt

Serves 4

**Butternut and pistou aren't obvious partners, but the
sweetness of squash goes very well with the garlicky basil
sauce. Experiment with different types of squash, such as
kabochka, the small Japanese squash with striped green skin.**

Preheat the oven to 400°F (200°C) Gas 6.

To make the pistou, put the oil, garlic, basil leaves, and a pinch of salt in
a small food processor. Whizz until well blended. Transfer to a small bowl.
Alternatively, to prepare without a machine, crush the garlic finely, then mix
with the oil and salt.

Trim the stem from the squash and cut in half lengthwise. Scoop out the
seeds. Arrange the squash halves in a roasting pan and sprinkle with salt.
Brush generously with the pistou, letting it well up a bit in the cavity.

Roast the squash in the preheated oven for about 40–45 minutes, until just
browned at the edges and tender when pierced with a knife. Serve hot, with
the remaining pistou on the side as a spooning sauce.

sweet things

tropical fruits in lime and chile syrup

1 large ripe papaya (pawpaw)

1 large ripe mango

1 ripe pineapple

2 star fruit or kiwi fruit, thinly sliced

For the lime and chile syrup:

½ cup/125 g sugar

thinly pared peel of 2 limes

freshly squeezed juice of
up to 1 lime

1 mild to hot fresh green or red chile,
seeded and finely diced

Serves 6

The aromatic sharpness of lime and the heat of chile bring out the sweetness and scent of exotic fruits such as papaya, mango, and pineapple. Even star fruit, a pretty but often uninspiring fruit, yields to this treatment.

To make the syrup, put the sugar and ½ cup/125 ml water in a small saucepan set over low heat and stir to dissolve the sugar.

Meanwhile, put the shreds of lime peel in a heatproof bowl and cover with boiling water. Let stand for 5 minutes, drain and repeat, then drain well.

When the sugar has dissolved, boil the syrup for 3–4 minutes until it thickens slightly, but do not let it burn. Let cool a little, then stir in the lime peel, followed by sufficient lime juice to make a sweet-sour syrup. Add about 1 teaspoon chile and set aside. Taste after 10 minutes and add more chile to taste, but remember that the chile will get hotter as the syrup cools.

To prepare the fruits, peel and pit the papaya and cut into slices. Peel, seed, and slice the mango. Peel, core, and thinly slice the pineapple. Arrange all the fruit on a platter or on individual plates. Trickle the syrup over the top, cover and chill for at least 30 minutes before serving.

peaches in lemon, bay leaf, and vanilla syrup

1¾ cups/175 g sugar

1 vanilla bean/pod, split lengthwise

3 fresh bay leaves

3 strips of lemon peel from 1 lemon

1–2 tablespoons freshly squeezed lemon juice

6 ripe white or yellow peaches, halved and pitted

non-dairy vegan ice cream, to serve (optional)

Serves 6

Nothing says summer more than a perfect, juicy ripe peach. Unfortunately, peaches like that are rare, but heat, sugar and flavorings such as lemon, bay, and real vanilla you can transform the most lacklustre fruit into something delicious.

Put the sugar in a heavy-based saucepan with 2½ cups/625 ml water and heat gently, stirring all the time to dissolve the sugar. Add the vanilla bean/pod, bay leaves, and the strips of lemon peel.

Let the syrup simmer for 5 minutes, then add the peaches, cut-side up. Poach them gently (the liquid should merely bubble occasionally) for 5–8 minutes. Test them with the tip of a pointed knife. When tender, remove the peaches carefully with a slotted spoon and, when cool enough, slip off the skin.

Meanwhile, reduce the liquid by fast boiling until it thickens slightly and becomes syrupy. Add the lemon juice to taste. Let cool, then pour the syrup over the peaches, tucking in the vanilla bean/pod, bay leaves, and lemon peel. When cold, cover and chill.

lemon, thyme, and green tea sorbet with pistachio cookies

3 green tea teabags

1 cup/200 g sugar

1 tablespoon fresh thyme sprigs, preferably lemon thyme

thinly pared zest of 2 lemons

freshly squeezed juice
of up to 1½ lemons

For the pistachio cookies:

1 cup/115 g shelled pistachios, lightly toasted in a dry skillet/frying pan and roughly chopped

3 cups/375 g whole-wheat pastry flour/wholemeal bread flour

½ teaspoon baking soda/bicarbonate of soda

½ teaspoon ground cinnamon

½ teaspoon sea salt

⅔ cup safflower/sunflower oil

⅔ cup/165 ml maple syrup

1 teaspoon vanilla extract

½ teaspoon almond extract

an ice cream machine (optional)
2 baking sheets, lightly oiled

Serves 6–8

You can experiment with different ingredients with this delightfully elegant herby sorbet. Try Earl Grey tea with lemon balm or jasmine tea with lemon and ginger. Leftover cookies can be stored in an airtight container for up to 1 week.

To make the sorbet, put the teabags in a bowl and pour over 2 cups/500 ml cold water, cover and leave overnight. The next day, dissolve the sugar in 1 cup/250 ml water in a saucepan over low heat and bring to a boil. Take off the heat and pour into a heatproof bowl, then add the thyme and lemon peel. Let the syrup cool, cover, then chill in the refrigerator overnight.

Strain both mixtures into a bowl and stir in lemon juice to taste. Chill, then churn in an ice cream machine according to the manufacturer's instructions, until frozen. Alternatively, turn into a freezerproof container to make a shallow layer and freeze until hard around the edges. Turn into a food processor and process until smooth. Repeat the freezing and processing once more, then allow to freeze firm. Let the sorbet soften in the refrigerator for 15–20 minutes, then serve with a few cookies for each person, if liked.

To make the cookies, preheat the oven to 375°F (190°C) Gas 5. In a large bowl, sift together the flour, baking soda, cinnamon, and salt. In another bowl, combine the oil, maple syrup, vanilla and almond extracts, and whisk well. Add the wet ingredients to the dry ingredients and stir well to combine. Fold in the toasted pistachios. Using your hands, form the dough into 1-inch/2.5 cm balls. Put the balls on the prepared baking sheets and flatten them slightly. Bake in the preheated oven for 10–12 minutes, or until lightly browned on the bottom. Let cool on the baking sheets for a few minutes, then transfer to a wire rack to cool completely. Store in an airtight container.

cranberry and raspberry jellies

1½ x 6-g envelopes (2¼ teaspoons) of Vege-gel

2 cups/500 ml cranberry juice

1½ tablespoons sugar

8 cloves

1 cinnamon stick

6 slices fresh ginger

1 cup/125 g fresh raspberries

vanilla-flavored soy yogurt, to serve (optional)

Serves 4

This jewel-like dessert is easy to make and very refreshing to eat. Cranberry juice is packed full of Vitamin C so if you're feeling under the weather one of these will give you a boost.

Sprinkle the Vege-gel into ¾ cup/200 ml of the cranberry juice and stir to dissolve. Simmer the remaining cranberry juice with the sugar and spices as above, then stir in the dissolved Vege-gel. Let cool.

Divide the raspberries between 4 glasses and strain the cooled jelly on top. Cover with plastic wrap/clingfilm and chill in the refrigerator for about 3 hours or until set. Serve the jellies with a dollop of vanilla-flavored soy yogurt on top, if liked.

Variation:

You can make this jelly with many other combinations of juice and fruit so do experiment to find one that you like. Try apple juice with blueberries or pineapple juice with chunks of fresh peach.

summer berry pudding

1 lb./450 g fresh or frozen mixed red berries, thawed if frozen

2 tablespoons maple syrup or agave nectar

½ cup/125 ml red wine

½ cup/125 ml water

1 cinnamon stick, bruised

8 slices multi-grain day-old bread, crusts removed

1 teaspoon arrowroot (optional)

soy yogurt or vegan sour cream (such as Tofutti Sour Supreme), to serve (optional)

a 2-cup/475-ml capacity bowl

Serves 4

Now that frozen summer fruits are readily available in most supermarkets, you can enjoy this treat all year round. It's a great dessert for entertaining as it's simple to but looks very impressive. Serve with soy yogurt or vegan sour cream.

If you are using fresh fruit, lightly rinse and let dry. Put the berries, maple syrup, red wine, water, and cinnamon stick in a medium saucepan and gently simmer over low heat for 5 minutes, until the berries are plump and slightly softened. Remove from the heat and let cool. Discard the cinnamon.

Cut 6 slices of bread into triangles and use them to line the base and sides of the bowl. Overlap the bread so it completely covers the bowl, leaving no gaps. Reserve the remaining 2 slices of bread to cover the top of the pudding. Spoon a little of the berry juice evenly over the bread in the bowl to moisten it. Fill the bowl with the berries, using a slotted spoon. Pack the fruit down with the back of a spoon, taking care not to squash the fruit too much. Cut the remaining 2 slices of bread into triangles. Put these on top of the fruit to make a lid. Reserve any remaining berry juice.

Cover the bowl with plastic wrap/clingfilm, put a small plate or saucer on top, then put weights on the plate to press it down onto the pudding. Leave in the refrigerator overnight.

Remove the weights, plate, and plastic wrap/clingfilm. Put a large plate upside down on top of the bowl. Carefully invert the bowl and plate, then gently remove the bowl.

Put the reserved juice in a saucepan and heat gently. If necessary, gently drizzle the sauce over any parts of the pudding that are not a consistent colour. Serve with dollops of soy yogurt or vegan sour cream, if using.

sticky Thai rice with fresh mango

2 cups/400 g sticky (glutinous) rice*

1¼ cups/300 ml coconut milk

2 tablespoons sugar

½ teaspoon salt

4 ripe mangoes

2 tablespoons coconut cream,
to serve

Serves 4

Sticky rice with fresh mango is probably Thailand's favourite sweet dish. Remember that sticky rice must be soaked for at least 3 hours or overnight, before steaming for 30 minutes or so.

Soak the rice in sufficient water to cover for at least 3 hours or overnight. Drain and rinse thoroughly. Line the perforated part of a steamer with a double thickness of cheesecloth/muslin and add the soaked rice. Heat water in the bottom of the steamer to boiling, then steam the rice over moderate heat for 30 minutes. Use the rice while still warm.

Put the coconut milk and sugar in a small saucepan and heat gently, stirring all the time, until the sugar has dissolved. Do not let it reach a boil. Stir in the salt and the warm sticky rice and set aside.

To prepare the mangoes, cut the 2 cheeks off each one, as close to the pit as possible. Cut each cheek into 4–6 long wedges, cutting through the flesh but not through the skin. Peel back and discard the skin.

Spoon the sticky rice into small bowls, add a few slices of mango, then trickle the coconut cream over the top. Serve warm or cold, as preferred.

*Note: Sticky rice is also used throughout Thailand to make sweet dishes, and it is milled into rice flour which is bought ready-ground. As its name implies, it is the opposite of light and fluffy, being thick and almost porridgy. Sticky rice cannot be cooked in an electric rice-steamer and must be soaked before cooking.

Madeira-roasted figs with pine nuts

8 fresh figs

⅓ cup/100 ml Madeira

3 tablespoons pine nuts

⅓ cup/75 g dark muscovado sugar

½ cup/200 g vanilla-flavored soy yogurt

Serves 4

Figs roasted in the oven with a splash of warming alcohol positively ooze succulence and sweetness. The vanilla soy yogurt becomes gorgeously fudgy when sprinkled with rich muscovado sugar.

Preheat the oven to 400°F (200°C) Gas 6.

Cut the stalks off the figs and cut a cross in the top about one-third of the way through. Stand them in an ovenproof dish, pour over the Madeira and scatter with the pine nuts and half the sugar. Bake in the preheated oven for 20–25 minutes, basting occasionally.

Spoon the soy yogurt into 4 bowls and scatter with the remaining sugar. Leave to stand for 10 minutes until it absorbs the sugar and turns slightly fudgy in texture.

When the figs are cooked and on the verge of collapsing, transfer them to serving bowls, add a dollop of fudgy soy yogurt and pour the hot sticky juices over the top.

baked apples and pears with dried fruit and hazelnuts

2 apples, preferably Cox or Braeburn

1 just-ripe pear, preferably Conference

1 oz./25 g whole blanched hazelnuts, coarsely chopped

6 soft prunes, chopped

4–5 dried figs, chopped

a pinch of ground cinnamon

4 tablespoons vegan margarine

4 tablespoons maple syrup or agave nectar

soy yogurt or non-dairy vegan soy ice cream, to serve (optional)

Serves 2

Baked fruit may seem old-fashioned, but not these, especially if you use a crisp eating apple. As well as being perhaps the easiest baked pudding there is to make, it tastes heavenly and perhaps the easiest cooked pudding you will ever make.

Preheat the oven to 400°F (200°C) Gas 6.

Peel the apples. If necessary, trim the bottom slightly so they sit flat. Remove the cores with a small knife or a corer. Using a small spoon, scrape out some apple to make space for more stuffing. Don't go all the way down to the bottom. Peel the pear, halve and scoop out the core.

Put the hazelnuts, prunes, and figs in a small bowl and stir well.

Arrange the apples and pears in an ovenproof dish. Stuff the nut mixture into the apple and pear cavities, mounding it at the top. Top each with a light sprinkling of cinnamon, 1 tablespoon margarine, and trickle over a teaspoon or so of maple syryp. Cover with foil.

Bake in the preheated oven for 20 minutes, then remove the foil and continue baking until just golden, about 10–15 minutes more. Divide the apples and pears carefully between serving plates and pour over any pan juices. Serve warm, with a dollop of soy yogurt or soy ice cream, if liked.

sweet potato and plantain spiced fritters

2 large sweet potatoes
2 plantains or under-ripe bananas
vegetable oil, for deep-frying

For the frothy batter:
2 cups/275 g all-purpose/plain flour
½ teaspoon freshly grated nutmeg
2 teaspoons ground cinnamon
about 1¾ cups/425 ml sparkling water
unrefined demerara sugar, to sprinkle

Serves 6–8

A Caribbean idea with its African roots in evidence. Sweet potatoes are great fritter vegetables, melting in your mouth with creamy sweetness. If you can find plantains snap them up, otherwise, under-ripe bananas can be substituted.

To make the batter, put the flour, nutmeg, and cinnamon into a large bowl and stir well. Make a well in the center and gradually whisk in enough sparkling water to make a smooth batter, thick enough to coat the back of a spoon. Cover with a kitchen towel and set aside for 20 minutes.

Cut the sweet potatoes into ½-inch/1.5 cm slices, then cut in half (you should have about 28 half-moon pieces). Cut the plantains or bananas into 1-inch/2.5 cm slices (about 10), because they will cook much faster.

Fill a deep saucepan one-third full of oil and heat to 375°F (190°C) or until a cube of bread browns in 30 seconds. Working in batches and using tongs, dip a piece of plantain or banana into the batter, coat well, then slide it into the hot oil—do not overcrowd the pan. Fry until golden brown all over. Remove with a slotted spoon, drain in a colander lined with paper towels, then transfer to a serving plate and keep them warm while you cook the sweet potatoes, again in batches.

Sprinkle with sugar and serve while hot and crispy.

oaty plum crumbles

1½ lbs./750 g ripe plums, pitted and sliced

1–2 tablespoons soft light brown (muscovado) sugar

non-dairy vegan soy ice cream, to serve (optional)

For the crumble topping:

¾ cup/100 g whole-wheat/wholemeal flour, preferably stoneground

½ teaspoon baking powder

3 tablespoons vegan margarine

⅓ cup/70 g soft dark brown sugar

⅔ cup/80 g whole rolled oats (jumbo)

¼ teaspoon freshly grated nutmeg

brown sugar, for sprinkling

4 individual ramekins

Serves 4

Plums, like cherries, apples and pears, are a particularly good fruit for baking. The crumble topping is made with jumbo oats, which become deliciously crunchy and make a nice contrast with the sweet fruit hidden underneath.

Preheat the oven to 350°F (180°C) Gas 4.

Put the plums, sugar, and 4 tablespoons water in a large saucepan. Heat until simmering, then simmer for 10–15 minutes, until the plums are just cooked and soft.

Meanwhile, to make the crumble topping, put the flour in a mixing bowl, add the margarine and rub it in with the tips of your fingers. The mixture should resemble bread crumbs. Add the sugar, oats, and nutmeg and mix well.

Divide the plums and their cooking liquid between the ramekins. Top with the crumble mixture, then sprinkle with a little sugar.

Bake in the preheated oven for 15–20 minutes, until the topping is golden and the fruit is bubbling. Serve warm with a scoop of soy ice cream, if liked.

Variation:

Replace the plums with apples, cherries, pears, apricots, peaches, or mixed red berries. For some extra spice, add 1 tablespoon of grated fresh ginger to the crumble mixture.

rhubarb and apple crumble

14 oz./400 g cooking apples, peeled, cored, and sliced

9 oz./250 g fresh rhubarb, sliced

4 tablespoons maple syrup or agave nectar

non-dairy vegan soy ice cream, to serve (optinal)

For the crumble topping:

2½ tablespoons vegan margarine

1 cup/125 g whole-wheat/wholemeal flour, preferably stoneground

⅓ cup/75 g soft light brown sugar

⅓ cup/40 g whole rolled oats (jumbo)

1 tablespoon whole blanched almonds, chopped

a shallow ovenproof baking dish, lightly greased

Serves 6

Whole rolled oats and almonds add extra texture to this deliciously nutty-tasting crumble topping. This is a great dessert when rhubarb is in season but could be replaced with tangy blackberries or fresh cranberries

Preheat the oven to 350°F (180°C) Gas 4.

Toss the fruit together with the maple syrup in the baking dish. Sprinkle with 4 tablespoons water, then cover with foil and bake in the preheated oven for 20 minutes.

Meanwhile, rub the margarine into the flour until the mixture resembles bread crumbs. Stir in the sugar, oats, and almonds. When the fruit is ready, scatter the crumble mix evenly on top, press down gently, then bake, uncovered, for 20 minutes until the topping is golden and the fruit juices are bubbling up around the edges. Serve with a scoop of soy ice cream, if liked.

peanut butter bars

4 tablespoons organic crunchy
peanut butter

4 tablespoons light corn syrup or
golden syrup

1½ cups/100 g whole rolled oats

⅓ cup/50 g golden raisins/sultanas

1 tablespoon whole-wheat/wholemeal
flour, preferably stoneground

a nonstick cake pan/tin,
6 x 9 inches/23 x 15 cm

Makes 8 bars

**Did you know that peanuts are in fact not nuts at all? They
are part of the legume family and therefore have many of the
beneficial properties of beans, including being high in fiber.
So it's no wonder these bars are so filling—they are almost
a meal in themselves!**

Preheat the oven to 375°F (190°C) Gas 5.

Put the peanut butter and corn syrup in a saucepan and heat very gently
until melted, about 3 minutes. Add the oats, golden raisins/sultanas, and
flour and stir well until thoroughly mixed and the mixture has the consistency
of bread crumbs.

Pour the mixture into the cake pan/tin and press in with the back of a
spoon. Bake in the preheated oven for 15 minutes. Score into bars or
squares with a knife while still warm, then allow to cool before cutting
through and removing the bars from the pan/tin. Once cool, the bars can
be stored in an airtight container for up to 2 weeks.

Variation:

Try adding chopped dried apricots or dried cranberries, instead
of the golden raisins/sultanas.

cherry and hazelnut cookies

6½ tablespoons light corn syrup or golden syrup

2½ tablespoons vegan margarine

½ cup/75 g whole rolled oats

½ cup plus 2 tablespoons/
75 g whole-wheat/wholemeal flour, preferably stoneground

1 teaspoon baking powder

⅛ teaspoon salt

a pinch of ground cinnamon

½ cup/50 g dried cherries

1 tablespoon toasted chopped hazelnuts

a baking sheet, lightly greased

Makes 14 cookies

These fruit and nut cookies are soft and chewy when freshly baked, then crisp up as they cool. The dried fruits and nuts can be varied to suit what's in your pantry.

Preheat the oven to 350°F (180°C) Gas 4.

Gently heat the corn syrup and margarine together in a small saucepan until melted. Let cool slightly.

Mix the oats, flour, cinnamon, cherries, and hazelnuts together in a bowl, then stir in the syrup mixture. Spoon 14 mounds of cookie dough onto the baking sheet, then flatten with the back of a spoon.

Bake in the preheated oven for 8–10 minutes, until golden brown and firm. Transfer to a wire rack to cool. Once cool, the cookies can be stored in an airtight container for up to 4 days.

choc-nut granola bars

8 tablespoons vegan margarine

½ cup/125 g light brown sugar

4 tablespoons light corn syrup or golden syrup

2 cups/200 g whole rolled oats

½ cup/25 g dry, unsweetened shredded/dessicated coconut

¼ cup/30 g whole blanched almonds,chopped

candied/glacé cherries (optional)

1½ oz./40 g non-dairy, vegan-friendly chocolate, roughly chopped

a nonstick cake pan/tin, 9 inches/ 23 cm square

Makes 12 granola bars

These extra-special granola bars studded with coconut, almonds, and chocolate and an indulgent treat.

Preheat the oven to 180°C (350°F) Gas 4.

Put the margarine, sugar, and corn syrup in a pan and set over low heat. Warm until the margarine melts and the sugar dissolves.

Remove from the heat and stir in the oats and coconut. Spoon into the pan/tin and press the mixture down evenly using the back of a spoon.

Scatter over the almonds, and cherries, and press lightly into the mixture. Bake in the preheated oven for 15–20 minutes. Remove from the oven and immediately sprinkle over the roughly chopped chocolate. Set aside until cool.

Score into bars or squares with a knife while still warm, then allow to cool before cutting through and removing the bars from the pan/tin. Once cool the bars will keep in an airtight container for 4–5 days.

drinks

Vitamin C boost

vitamin c boost juice

6 oranges
3 ruby grapefruit
3 cups/500 g strawberries
ice cubes, to serve

Makes 3–4 drinks

All three fruits here are a valuable source of vitamin C, so this tangy juice is perfect for an early morning boost.

Peel and chop the oranges and grapefruit, leaving some of the pith intact. (The white pith on citrus fruits is high in antioxidants so it's good to include in the juice for its health benefits.)

Hull the strawberries and press all the fruit through a juicer into a pitcher/jug. Serve poured over ice.

dairy-free breakfast smoothie

1 banana
1 small mango, about 14 oz./400 g
1 cup/125 g fresh or frozen blueberries
⅓ cup/50 g muesli
2 cups/500 ml apple juice

Makes 3 drinks

This delicious drink will definitely give you a boost of energy with its high-sugar fruit, but it also provides natural vitamins, minerals and fiber to sustain your energy levels until lunchtime.

Peel and chop the banana. To prepare the mango, slice down each side of the pit/stone and cut away the flesh from the skin. Put the banana and mango in a blender with the blueberries, muesli, and apple juice. Blend until smooth. Pour into glasses and serve immediately.

soy, sesame, and maple syrup smoothie

1 banana
2 tablespoons tahini
2 tablespoons maple syrup
1¼ cups/300 ml soy milk
1 cup/250 ml soy yogurt

Makes 2 drinks

You may find the inclusion of an ingredient such as tahini (sesame seed paste) strange in a smoothie, but it makes a delicious drink. Tahini helps boost calcium levels.

Peel the banana, chop the flesh, and put in a blender with the remaining ingredients. Blend until smooth. Pour into glasses and serve immediately.

pineapple and passion fruit soy shake

½ fresh pineapple
1 cup/250 ml passion fruit pulp (from about 8 large fruits)
1 cup/250 ml soy milk
4 scoops vanilla soy ice cream

Makes 3 drinks

A delicious combination of tropical fruits. When choosing a pineapple, pull one of the outside leaves; if ripe, they will pull away easily. Passion fruit pulp is also available in cans from larger supermarkets.

Peel the pineapple, discard the tough central core and chop the flesh. Put it in a blender with the passion fruit pulp, soy milk, and soy ice cream. Blend until smooth. Pour into glasses and serve immediately.

LEFT **Pineapple and passion fruit soy shake**
RIGHT **Soy, sesame, and maple syrup smoothie**

LEFT **Caribbean cruise**
FRONT **Creamy berry soy shake**
RIGHT **Peanut and carob protein smoothie**

Caribbean cruise

½ pineapple
1 small papaya, about 1 lb./450 g
1¼ cups/300 ml coconut milk
8 ice cubes

Makes 4 drinks

This smoothie is nutrient-dense to pick you up between meals, especially when you are craving sugar or hit an energy slump.

Peel the pineapple and discard the thick central core. Cut the flesh into chunks. Peel and halve the papaya, scoop out and discard the seeds and chop the flesh. Put the pineapple and papaya in a blender, add the coconut milk and ice cubes and blend until smooth. Pour into glasses and serve immediately.

creamy berry soy shake

1 cup/125 g raspberries
¾ cup/100 g blackberries
2 scoops vanilla soy ice cream
2 cups/500 ml soy milk

Makes 2–3 drinks

This is a thick and totally delicious fruit drink. You could substitute berry sorbet for the soy ice cream for a change.

Put all the ingredients together in a blender and blend until smooth. Pour into glasses and serve immediately.

peanut and carob protein smoothie

2 bananas
8 oz./250 g silken tofu
3 tablespoons smooth peanut butter
1 tablespoon maple syrup
2 teaspoons carob powder
1¼ cups/300 ml soy milk

Makes 2 drinks

This thick, heavy smoothie is very filling and provides a healthy snack or a meal in itself. Carob is a caffeine-free alternative to chocolate available from health-food stores.

Peel the bananas, chop the flesh and put in a blender. Add all of the remaining ingredients and blend until smooth. Pour into glasses and serve immediately.

carob and maple rice milk shake

2 cups/500 ml rice milk

2 tablespoons maple syrup

½ tablespoon carob powder or organic cocoa powder

4 scoops chocolate soy ice cream

Makes 2 drinks

Carob has quite a strong flavor that can be overpowering, but the addition of maple syrup helps balance it and imparts a lovely caramel taste to this drink. You can use organic cocoa powder instead of the carob powder, if you prefer.

Put all the ingredients in a blender and blend until smooth. Pour into glasses and serve immediately.

banana and granola soy smoothie

2 bananas

⅓ cup/50 g granola, plus extra to serve

2 cups/500 ml soy milk

½ cup/125 ml soy yogurt

1 teaspoon ground cinnamon, plus extra to dust

maple syrup or agave nectar, to serve

Makes 2–3 drinks

Sweet, nutty granola is combined here with the warm spiciness of the ground cinnamon to make a delicious treat in a glass.

Peel the bananas and chop the flesh. Put in a blender with the granola, soy milk, yogurt, and cinnamon and blend until smooth. Pour into glasses and serve topped with a little extra ground cinnamon, a sprinkling of granola, and a drizzle of syrup.

date, banana, and rice milk frappé

4 Medjool dates, pitted

½ cup/125 ml apple juice

2 bananas

1¼ cups/300 ml rice milk

Makes 2 drinks

Dates provide a quick energy boost and satisfy sugar cravings. Choose plump, soft dates such as the Medjool variety, which give the shake a delicious caramel flavor.

Put the dates and apple juice in a small saucepan, heat gently until boiling, then cover and simmer for 5 minutes until the dates have softened. Let cool completely. Transfer the dates and juice to a blender. Peel and chop the bananas, add them and the rice milk to the blender and blend until smooth. Pour into glasses and serve immediately.

Carob and maple
rice milk shake

Spiced Mango, coconut, and lime smoothie

malted strawberry oat shake

1 banana
2 cups/250 g strawberries
2 tablespoons oat bran
2 cups/500 ml oat milk
1 tablespoon malt extract

Makes 2 drinks

**This power-packed shake is great for kick-starting the day.
Oat bran adds a delicate nutty flavor and bulk to make a
satisfying drink.**

Peel the banana and chop the flesh. Hull the strawberries and put them and
the banana in a blender. Add the oat bran, oat milk, and malt extract and
blend until smooth. Pour into glasses and serve immediately.

spiced mango, coconut, and lime smoothie

1 large mango, about 1 lb. 4 oz./550 g
1⅔ cups/400 ml coconut milk
freshly squeezed juice of 1 lime
1 cup/250 ml freshly squeezed
orange juice
½ teaspoon ground allspice, plus
extra to dust

Makes 4 drinks

**Mango flesh becomes silky smooth when blended to make
a deliciously indulgent yet nutritious drink.**

To prepare the mango, slice down each side of the pit and cut away the
flesh from the skin. Put the flesh in a blender with the coconut milk, lime
juice, orange juice, and allspice and blend until smooth. Pour into glasses
and serve immediately, dusted with a little extra allspice.

index

recipe credits

Vatcharin Bhumichitr
deep-fried yellow bean balls
    with Thai-style sticky sauce
sticky rice with fresh mango

Tamsin Burnett-Hall
cherry and hazelnut oat cookies
cranberry and raspberry jellies
Italian cannellini bean and
    vegetable soup
Moroccan seven-vegetable
    tagine with quinoa
rhubarb and apple crumble
ribbon vegetable and hummus
    wraps
spicy bean burritos

Maxine Clark
falafel with avocado, tomato,
    and red onion salsa
marinated grilled eggplant with
    salmoriglio dressing
saffron potato salad with
    sun-dried tomatoes and
    caper and basil dressing
smoked eggplant dip
    (baba ghanoush)

Ross Dobson
barley risotto with spring greens
    and radicchio
cauliflower and Swiss chard
    salad
chickpea, tomato, and green
    bean minestrone
creamy vegetable and coconut
    cashew curry
eggplant, tomato, and red
    lentil curry
garlic and chile rice soup with
    wilted greens
grilled mixed vegetable platter
    with rice
miso with ramen noodles and
    stir-fried vegetables
orange vegetable pilau
paella of summer vine
    vegetables with almonds
pickled spring vegetable salad
    with marinated tofu
pan-roasted carrots with barley
    risotto
roasted vegetables with
    chickpeas
root vegetable ragu with spiced
    couscous
smoky hotpot of great northern
    beans
spiced cauliflower with red bell
    pepper and peas
spiced eggplant couscous
spicy Cajun mixed nuts
stir-fried tofu with crisp greens
    and mushrooms
sweet potato and coconut soup

with Thai pesto
tabbouleh with chickpeas and
    spring salad
tagliatelle with pan-fried
    pumpkin and red pepper oil
tempura of mixed vegetables
    with citrus dipping sauce
vegetable potsticker dumplings
    with orange dipping sauce

Clare Ferguson
fennel and orange salad with
    black olives
gazpacho
Italian bean dip
Provençal pickled beans
Spanish stuffed peppers

Manisha Gambhir Harkins
butternut squash soup with
    allspice and pine nuts
cashew salad with tamarind
    dressing
Indian vegetable fritters with
    green chutney
perfumed Persian rice pulow
sweet potato and plaintain
    spiced fritters
vegetable stir-fry with Szechuan
    peppercorns

Tonia George
Madeira-roasted figs with
    pine nuts
roast eggplant and red bell
    pepper soup with basil oil
summer vegetable and lemon
    broth

Brian Glover
lemon, thyme, and green tea
    sorbet with pistachio cookies
nutty rice salad with preserved
    lemon dressing
peaches in lemon, bay leaf, and
    vanilla syrup
tropical fruits in lime and chile
    syrup

Rachael Anne Hill
baked stuffed mushrooms
oaty plum crumbles
peanut butter bars
summer berry pudding

Jennifer Joyce
Lebanese hot red pepper and
    walnut dip (muhammara)

Caroline Marson
choc-nut granola bars

Jane Noraika
Calabrian-style baked potatoes
    and peppers

portobello mushrooms in lemon
    and olive oil
sesame sweet potato wedges
    with peanut dipping sauce
summer squash infused with
    mint and balsamic vinegar
tofu in a hot, sweet, and spicy
    infusion

Elsa Petersen-Schepelern
black rice salad with chile
    greens
couscous salad with chickpeas
    and artichokes
Greek horta salad with roast
    beets
Indian potato salad
Japanese tofu salad with
    sesame seeds
red salad with beet and
    cabbage
Tuscan panzanella

Louise Pickford
banana and granola soy
    smoothie
Caribbean cruise
carob and maple rice milk shake
creamy berry soy shake
dairy-free breakfast smoothie
date, banana, and rice milk
    frappé
malted strawberry oat shake
peanut and carob protein
    smoothie
pineapple and passion fruit
    soy shake
quick potato and vegetable
    curry
soy, sesame, and maple
    smoothie
spiced mango, coconut, and
    lime smoothie
vitamin c boost juice

Rena Salaman
Greek yellow split pea purée
imam bayildi
okra with dried limes
stuffed vine leaves

Jennie Shapter
mini spring rolls with chile
    dipping sauce

Fiona Smith
artichoke tarator
brown rice, hazelnut, and herb
    salad with kaffir lime dressing
five-bean salad with lemon and
    poppy seed dressing
green bean and chickpea salad
    with sesame dressing
grilled vegetable and almond
    couscous with herb dressing

guacamole
herb, red onion, and quinoa
    salad with preserved lemon
hummus
puy lentil and carrot pâté
ratatouille
rice noodle, carrot, and
    cabbage salad with Chinese
    five-spice dressing
roasted sweet potato and
    macadamia nut salad
roasted tomato and red bell
    pepper fattoush
tagine of root vegetables
    with prunes
tomato, avocado, and lime
    salad with crisp tortillas

Linda Tubby
baby leeks with chile bread
    crumbs
oven-roasted vegetables with
    rosemary, bay leaves, and
    garlic
singaras with fresh mango salsa
Turkish salad with mint and
    parsley

Laura Washburn
baked apples and pears with
    dried fruit and hazelnuts
butternut squash with pistou
grilled, chile-marinated zucchini
tourlou
zucchini and corn soup

photography credits

Key: a=above, b=below, r=right, l=left, c=center.

Martin Brigdale
Pages 3 left and center right,
21, 39, 82, 85, 158

Peter Cassidy
Pages 5, 25, 40, 48, 60,
63, 64, 71, 78, 81, 86,
97–106,130, 134, 142, 153,
154, 181, 207, 212

Nicki Dowey
Pages 185, 204, 215, 219

Richard Jung
Pages 1, 3 center left and
right, 4, 6, 10–17, 22, 30,
51, 67, 74, 77, 93, 94,
124–129, 133, 137, 138,
141, 146, 149, 157, 161,
166, 170–178, 182, 193,
195–200, 211

William Lingwood
Pages 52, 55, 150, 186,
189, 190

Diana Miller
Pages 9, 31, 43, 44, 47, 72,
73, 89, 90, 109–122, 145,
162, 165

Noel Murphy
Pages 36, 68

William Reavell
Pages 2, 18, 56, 59, 169,
194, 203, 208, 216, 221, 225

Yuki Sugiura
Pages 8, 26, 29

Ian Wallace
Pages 224, 226–234

Kate Whitaker
Pages 32, 35

Polly Wreford
Page 223